# Just The facts101
## Textbook Key Facts

Textbook Outlines, Highlights, and Practice Quizzes

---

## Interpersonal Communication

by Kory Floyd, 2nd Edition

All "Just the Facts101" Material Written or Prepared by Cram101 Publishing

---

Title Page

Cram101.com for Practice Tests

# WHY STOP HERE... THERE'S MORE ONLINE

With technology and experience, we've developed tools that make studying easier and efficient. Like this Cram101 textbook notebook, Cram101.com offers you the highlights from every chapter of your actual textbook. However, unlike this notebook, Cram101.com gives you practice tests for each of the chapters. You also get access to in-depth reference material for writing essays and papers.

By purchasing this book, you get 50% off the normal subscription free!. Just enter the promotional code **'DK73DW20820'** on the Cram101.com registration screen.

## CRAMIOI.COM FEATURES:

**Outlines & Highlights**
Just like the ones in this notebook, but with links to additional information.

**Integrated Note Taking**
Add your class notes to the Cram101 notes, print them and maximize your study time.

**Problem Solving**
Step-by-step walk throughs for math, stats and other disciplines.

**Practice Exams**
Five different test taking formats for every chapter.

**Easy Access**
Study any of your books, on any computer, anywhere.

**Unlimited Textbooks**
All the features above for virtually all your textbooks, just add them to your account at no additional cost.

Be sure to use the promo code above when registering on Cram101.com to get 50% off your membership fees.

## STUDYING MADE EASY

This Cram101 notebook is designed to make studying easier and increase your comprehension of the textbook material. Instead of starting with a blank notebook and trying to write down everything discussed in class lectures, you can use this Cram101 textbook notebook and annotate your notes along with the lecture.

*Our goal is to give you the best tools for success.*

For a supreme understanding of the course, pair your notebook with our online tools. Should you decide you prefer Cram101.com as your study tool,

*we'd like to offer you a trade...*

Our Trade In program is a simple way for us to keep our promise and provide you the best studying tools, regardless of where you purchased your Cram101 textbook notebook. As long as your notebook is in *Like New Condition\**, you can send it back to us and we will immediately give you a Cram101.com account free for 120 days!

## Let The *Trade In* Begin!

### THREE SIMPLE STEPS TO TRADE:

1. Go to www.cram101.com/tradein and fill out the packing slip information.
2. Submit and print the packing slip and mail it in with your Cram101 textbook notebook.
3. Activate your account after you receive your email confirmation.

\* Books must be returned in *Like New Condition*, meaning there is no damage to the book including, but not limited to; ripped or torn pages, markings or writing on pages, or folded / creased pages. Upon receiving the book, Cram101 will inspect it and reserves the right to terminate your free Cram101.com account and return your textbook notebook at the owners expense.

Cram101

# cram101
## LEARNING SYSTEM

*"Just the Facts101"* is a Cram101 publication and tool designed to give you all the facts from your textbooks. Visit Cram101.com for the full practice test for each of your chapters for virtually any of your textbooks.

Cram101 has built custom study tools specific to your textbook. We provide all of the factual testable information and unlike traditional study guides, we will never send you back to your textbook for more information.

*YOU WILL NEVER HAVE TO HIGHLIGHT A BOOK AGAIN!*

### Cram101 StudyGuides
All of the information in this StudyGuide is written specifically for your textbook. We include the key terms, places, people, and concepts... the information you can expect on your next exam!

### Want to take a practice test?
Throughout each chapter of this StudyGuide you will find links to cram101.com where you can select specific chapters to take a complete test on, or you can subscribe and get practice tests for up to 12 of your textbooks, along with other exclusive cram101.com tools like problem solving labs and reference libraries.

### Cram101.com
Only cram101.com gives you the outlines, highlights, and PRACTICE TESTS specific to your textbook. Cram101.com is an online application where you'll discover study tools designed to make the most of your limited study time.

By purchasing this book, you get 50% off the normal subscription free!. Just enter the promotional code **'DK73DW20820'** on the Cram101.com registration screen.

*www.Cram101.com*

Copyright © 2012 by Cram101, Inc. All rights reserved.
"Just the FACTS101"®, "Cram101"® and "Never Highlight a Book Again!"® are registered trademarks of Cram101, Inc.
ISBN(s): 9781478426820. PUBX-1.20121214

Learning System

Interpersonal Communication
Kory Floyd, 2nd

# CONTENTS

1. About Communication ............... 5
2. Culture and Gender ............... 14
3. Communication and the Self ............... 23
4. Interpersonal Perception ............... 32
5. Language ............... 39
6. Nonverbal Communication ............... 51
7. Listening ............... 62
8. Emotion ............... 70
9. Interpersonal Communication in Friendships and Professional Relationships ............... 77
10. Interpersonal Communication in Romantic and Family Relationships ............... 84
11. Interpersonal Conflict ............... 91
12. Deceptive Communication ............... 98

# Chapter 1. About Communication

CHAPTER OUTLINE: KEY TERMS, PEOPLE, PLACES, CONCEPTS

- Procedural
- FINANCIAL
- Spelling bee
- Natural language
- Internet
- Communication
- Spirituality
- Human communication
- Encoding
- Interaction
- Interpersonal communication
- Nonverbal
- Nonverbal communication
- Online
- Feedback
- Prevention
- Transaction
- Mass communication
- Small group

# Chapter 1. About Communication
CHAPTER OUTLINE: KEY TERMS, PEOPLE, PLACES, CONCEPTS

- Small group communication
- Personal network
- Cyberspace Communications
- Cognitive complexity

CHAPTER HIGHLIGHTS & NOTES: KEY TERMS, PEOPLE, PLACES, CONCEPTS

| | |
|---|---|
| Procedural | A Procedural is a cross-genre type of literature, film, or television program involving a sequence of technical detail. A documentary film may be written in a procedural style to heighten narrative interest.<br><br>Types<br><br>Television<br><br>Fiction<br><br>In television, 'procedural' specifically refers to a genre of programs in which a problem is introduced, investigated and solved all within the same episode. |
| FINANCIAL | FINANCIAL is the weekly English-language newspaper with offices in Tbilisi, Georgia and Kiev, Ukraine. Published by Intelligence Group LLC, FINANCIAL is focused on opinion leaders and top business decision-makers; It's about world's largest companies, investing, careers, and small business. It is distributed in Georgia and Ukraine. |
| Spelling bee | A spelling bee is a competition where contestants, usually children, are asked to spell English words. The concept is thought to have originated in the United States. Today, National Spelling Bee competitions for English are held in the United States, United Kingdom, Australia, New Zealand, Canada, Indonesia and India among others. |

# Chapter 1. About Communication

CHAPTER HIGHLIGHTS & NOTES: KEY TERMS, PEOPLE, PLACES, CONCEPTS

| | |
|---|---|
| Natural language | In the philosophy of language, a natural language is any language which arises in an unpremeditated fashion as the result of the innate facility for language possessed by the human intellect. A natural language is typically used for communication, and may be spoken, signed, or written. Natural language is distinguished from constructed languages and formal languages such as computer-programming languages or the 'languages' used in the study of formal logic, especially mathematical logic. |
| Internet | The Internet is a global system of interconnected computer networks that use the standard Internet Protocol Suite (TCP/IP) to serve billions of users worldwide. It is a network of networks that consists of millions of private, public, academic, business, and government networks, of local to global scope, that are linked by a broad array of electronic, wireless and optical networking technologies. The Internet carries a vast range of information resources and services, such as the inter-linked hypertext documents of the World Wide Web (WWW) and the infrastructure to support electronic mail. |
| Communication | Communication is the activity of conveying information. Communication has been derived from the Latin word 'communis', meaning to share. Communication requires a sender, a message, and an intended recipient, although the receiver need not be present or aware of the sender's intent to communicate at the time of communication; thus communication can occur across vast distances in time and space. |
| Spirituality | Spirituality can refer to an ultimate or an alleged immaterial reality; an inner path enabling a person to discover the essence of his/her being; or the 'deepest values and meanings by which people live.' Spiritual practices, including meditation, prayer and contemplation, are intended to develop an individual's inner life; spiritual experience includes that of connectedness with a larger reality, yielding a more comprehensive self; with other individuals or the human community; with nature or the cosmos; or with the divine realm. Spirituality is often experienced as a source of inspiration or orientation in life. It can encompass belief in immaterial realities or experiences of the immanent or transcendent nature of the world. |
| Human communication | Human communication, is the field dedicated to understanding how people communicate:•with themselves: intrapersonal communication •expression: body language•another person: interpersonal communication•within groups: group dynamics•within organizations: organizational communication•across cultures: cross-cultural communicationImportant figures •Colin Cherry•Wendell Johnson•Marshall McLuhan•Albert Mehrabian•Carl Rogers•Norbert Wiener. |
| Encoding | Encoding is the process of transforming information from one format into another. The opposite operation is called decoding. This is often used in many digital devices<br><br>There are a number of more specific meanings that apply in certain contexts: |

# Chapter 1. About Communication

CHAPTER HIGHLIGHTS & NOTES: KEY TERMS, PEOPLE, PLACES, CONCEPTS

|  |  |
|---|---|
|  | · encoding (in cognition) is a basic perceptual process of interpreting incoming stimuli; technically speaking, it is a complex, multi-stage process of converting relatively objective sensory input (e.g., light, sound) into subjectively meaningful experience. |
| Interaction | Interaction is a kind of action that occurs as two or more objects have an effect upon one another. The idea of a two-way effect is essential in the concept of interaction, as opposed to a one-way causal effect. A closely related term is interconnectivity, which deals with the interactions of interactions within systems: combinations of many simple interactions can lead to surprising emergent phenomena. |
| Interpersonal communication | Interpersonal communication is usually defined by communication scholars in numerous ways, usually describing participants who are dependent upon one another. It can involve one on one conversations or individuals interacting with many people within a society. It helps us understand how and why people behave and communicate in different ways to construct and negotiate a social reality. |
| Nonverbal | Nonverbal communications (NVC) is usually understood as the process of communication through sending and receiving wordless messages. i.e, language is not one source of communication, there are other means also. NVC can be communicated through gestures and touch (Haptic communication), by body language or posture, by facial expression and eye contact. |
| Nonverbal communication | Nonverbal communication is usually understood as the process of communication through sending and receiving wordless (mostly visual) messages between people. Messages can be communicated through gestures and touch, by body language or posture, by facial expression and eye contact. Nonverbal messages could also be communicated through material exponential; meaning, objects or artifacts(such as clothing, hairstyles or architecture). |
| Online | The terms online and offline (also on-line and off-line) have specific meanings with respect to computer technology and telecommunication. In general, 'online' indicates a state of connectivity, while 'offline' indicates a disconnected state. In common usage, 'online' often refers to the Internet or the World Wide Web. |
| Feedback | Feedback describes the situation when output from an event or phenomenon in the past will influence the same event/phenomenon in the present or future. When an event is part of a chain of cause-and-effect that forms a circuit or loop, then the event is said to 'feed back' into itself.<br><br>Feedback is also a synonym for: |

# Chapter 1. About Communication

CHAPTER HIGHLIGHTS & NOTES: KEY TERMS, PEOPLE, PLACES, CONCEPTS

| | |
|---|---|
| Prevention | Prevention refers to:<br><br>· Preventive medicine · Hazard Prevention, the process of risk study and elimination and mitigation in emergency management · Risk Prevention · Risk management · Preventive maintenance · Crime Prevention<br><br>· Prevention, an album by Scottish band De Rosa · Prevention a magazine about health in the United States · Prevent (company), a textile company from Slovenia · Prevent (campaign), an anti-radicalization program in the United Kingdom |
| Transaction | In data mining, a transaction is an element of a family of a set of items. In other words, the transaction is a subset of the set of items.<br><br>Let I be a set of items and $T$ be a family of sets over I. |
| Mass communication | Mass communication is the term used to describe the academic study of the various means by which individuals and entities relay information through mass media to large segments of the population at the same time. It is usually understood to relate to newspaper and magazine publishing, radio, television and film, as these are used both for disseminating news and for advertising. |
| Small group | Small-group Communication refers to the nature of communication that occurs in groups that are between 3 and 12 to 20 individuals . small group communication generally takes place in a context that mixes interpersonal communication interactions with social clustering.<br><br>The first important research study of small group communication was performed by social psychologist Robert Bales and published in a series of books and articles in the early and mid 1950s . |
| Small group communication | Small-group Communication refers to the nature of communication that occurs in groups that are between 3 and 12 to 20 individuals . small group communication generally takes place in a context that mixes interpersonal communication interactions with social clustering.<br><br>The first important research study of small group communication was performed by social psychologist Robert Bales and published in a series of books and articles in the early and mid 1950s . |
| Personal network | A personal network is a set of human contacts known to an individual, with whom that individual would expect to interact at intervals to support a given set of activities. |

# Chapter 1. About Communication

## CHAPTER HIGHLIGHTS & NOTES: KEY TERMS, PEOPLE, PLACES, CONCEPTS

| | |
|---|---|
| | Personal networks are intended to be mutually beneficial--extending the concept of teamwork beyond the immediate peer group. The term is usually encountered in the workplace, though it could apply equally to other pursuits outside work. |
| Cyberspace Communications | Cyberspace Communications is a non-profit organization located in Ann Arbor, Michigan that promotes free speech through its anonymous access Unix system, Grex. The organization gained wide attention as the lead plaintiff in a successful suit to invalidate Michigan Public Act 33 of 1999 (The Child Online Protection Act). |
| | Cyberspace Communications was formed to govern the public access Unix system Grex. |
| Cognitive complexity | Cognitive complexity describes cognition along a simplicity-complexity axis. It is the subject of academic study in fields including personal construct psychology, organisational theory and human-computer interaction. |
| | First proposed by James Bieri in 1955. |

## CHAPTER QUIZ: KEY TERMS, PEOPLE, PLACES, CONCEPTS

1. _____ is usually understood as the process of communication through sending and receiving wordless (mostly visual) messages between people. Messages can be communicated through gestures and touch, by body language or posture, by facial expression and eye contact. Nonverbal messages could also be communicated through material exponential; meaning, objects or artifacts(such as clothing, hairstyles or architecture).

    a. Paralanguage
    b. Nonverbal communication
    c. Reply
    d. Sigh

2. . A _____ is a cross-genre type of literature, film, or television program involving a sequence of technical detail. A documentary film may be written in a _____ style to heighten narrative interest.

    Types

    Television

    Fiction

# Chapter 1. About Communication

CHAPTER QUIZ: KEY TERMS, PEOPLE, PLACES, CONCEPTS

In television, '_____' specifically refers to a genre of programs in which a problem is introduced, investigated and solved all within the same episode.

a. Prose poetry
b. Prosimetrum
c. Psychological novel
d. Procedural

3. In data mining, a _____ is an element of a family of a set of items. In other words, the _____ is a subset of the set of items.

Let I be a set of items and $T$ be a family of sets over I.

a. Weather Data Mining
b. Web mining
c. Transaction
d. DataRush Technology

4. _____ is the weekly English-language newspaper with offices in Tbilisi, Georgia and Kiev, Ukraine. Published by Intelligence Group LLC, _____ is focused on opinion leaders and top business decision-makers; It's about world's largest companies, investing, careers, and small business. It is distributed in Georgia and Ukraine.

a. Baka
b. Prosimetrum
c. FINANCIAL
d. Psychological thriller

5. _____ is the term used to describe the academic study of the various means by which individuals and entities relay information through mass media to large segments of the population at the same time. It is usually understood to relate to newspaper and magazine publishing, radio, television and film, as these are used both for disseminating news and for advertising.

a. Baka
b. Sentimental poetry
c. Sentimentalism
d. Mass communication

**ANSWER KEY**
**Chapter 1. About Communication**

1. b
2. d
3. c
4. c
5. d

## You can take the complete Chapter Practice Test

**for Chapter 1. About Communication**
on all key terms, persons, places, and concepts.

## Online 99 Cents

### http://www.epub21.1.20820.1.cram101.com/

Use www.Cram101.com for all your study needs

including Cram101's online interactive problem solving labs in

chemistry, statistics, mathematics, and more.

# Chapter 2. Culture and Gender

CHAPTER OUTLINE: KEY TERMS, PEOPLE, PLACES, CONCEPTS

| | Restrictive |
| | Social network |
| | Othello error |
| | Ethnocentrism |
| | Spelling bee |
| | Abstraction |
| | Values |
| | Norm |
| | Clubflyer |
| | Communication |
| | Interpersonal communication |
| | Intrapersonal communication |
| | Nonverbal |
| | Nonverbal communication |
| | Online |
| | Femininity |
| | Gender role |
| | Metrosexual |
| | FINANCIAL |

## Chapter 2. Culture and Gender

CHAPTER OUTLINE: KEY TERMS, PEOPLE, PLACES, CONCEPTS

_____ | Heterosexuality
_____ | Intersex
_____ | Sexual attraction
_____ | Prevention
_____ | Asexuality
_____ | Linguistic

CHAPTER HIGHLIGHTS & NOTES: KEY TERMS, PEOPLE, PLACES, CONCEPTS

| | |
|---|---|
| Restrictive | In semantics, a modifier is said to be restrictive (or defining) if it restricts the reference of its head. For example, in 'the red car is fancier than the blue one', red and blue are restrictive, because they restrict which cars car and one are referring to. ('The car is fancier than the one' would make little sense). |
| Social network | A social network is a social structure made up of a set of actors (such as individuals or organizations) and the dyadic ties between these actors (such as relationships, connections, or interactions). A social network perspective is employed to model the structure of a social group, how this structure influences other variables, or how structures change over time. The study of these structures uses methods in social network analysis to identify influential nodes, local and global structures, and network dynamics. |
| Othello error | Othello error occurs when a suspicious observer discounts cues of truthfulness, given the observer's need to conform his/her observations of suspicions of deception. Essentially Othello error occurs 'when the lie catcher fails to consider that a truthful person who is under stress may appear to be lying.' (Ekman, 1985).<br><br>The term relates to the Shakespeare play in which Othello misinterprets Desdemona's reaction to Cassio's death. |

# Chapter 2. Culture and Gender

CHAPTER HIGHLIGHTS & NOTES: KEY TERMS, PEOPLE, PLACES, CONCEPTS

| | |
|---|---|
| Ethnocentrism | Ethnocentrism is the tendency to believe that one's ethnic or cultural group is centrally important, and that all other groups are measured in relation to one's own. The ethnocentric individual will judge other groups relative to his or her own particular ethnic group or culture, especially with concern to language, behavior, customs, and religion. These ethnic distinctions and sub-divisions serve to define each ethnicity's unique cultural identity. |
| Spelling bee | A spelling bee is a competition where contestants, usually children, are asked to spell English words. The concept is thought to have originated in the United States. Today, National Spelling Bee competitions for English are held in the United States, United Kingdom, Australia, New Zealand, Canada, Indonesia and India among others. |
| Abstraction | Abstraction is a process by which higher concepts are derived from the usage and classification of literal ('real' or 'concrete') concepts, first principles, or other methods. 'An abstraction' is the product of this process - a concept that acts as a super-categorical noun for all subordinate concepts, and connects any related concepts as a group, field, or category.<br><br>Abstractions may be formed by reducing the information content of a concept or an observable phenomenon, typically to retain only information which is relevant for a particular purpose. |
| Values | The values embodied in cultural heritage are identified in order to assess significance, prioritize resources, and inform conservation decision-making. It is recognised that values may compete and change over time, and that heritage may have different meanings for different stakeholders.<br><br>Alois Riegl is credited with developing Ruskin's concept of 'voicefulness' into a systematic categorization of the different values of a monument. |
| Norm | Norms are sentences or concepts with practical, i. e. action-oriented (rather than descriptive, explanatory, or expressive) import. Norms imply 'ought'-type statements or assertions, in distinction to descriptions which provide 'is'-type statements or assertions. Some common sentences that are norms include commands, permissions, and prohibitions. |
| Clubflyer | A Clubflyer or flyer (also spelled flier or called handbill) is a single page leaflet advertising a nightclub, event, service, community communication. |
| Communication | Communication is the activity of conveying information. Communication has been derived from the Latin word 'communis', meaning to share. Communication requires a sender, a message, and an intended recipient, although the receiver need not be present or aware of the sender's intent to communicate at the time of communication; thus communication can occur across vast distances in time and space. |

# Chapter 2. Culture and Gender

CHAPTER HIGHLIGHTS & NOTES: KEY TERMS, PEOPLE, PLACES, CONCEPTS

| | |
|---|---|
| Interpersonal communication | Interpersonal communication is usually defined by communication scholars in numerous ways, usually describing participants who are dependent upon one another. It can involve one on one conversations or individuals interacting with many people within a society. It helps us understand how and why people behave and communicate in different ways to construct and negotiate a social reality. |
| Intrapersonal communication | Intrapersonal communication is language use or thought internal to the communicator. It can be useful to envision intrapersonal communication occurring in the mind of the individual in a model which contains a sender, receiver, and feedback loop.<br><br>Although successful communication is generally defined as being between two or more individuals, issues concerning the useful nature of communicating with oneself and problems concerning communication with non-sentient entities such as computers have made some argue that this definition is too narrow. |
| Nonverbal | Nonverbal communications (NVC) is usually understood as the process of communication through sending and receiving wordless messages. i.e, language is not one source of communication, there are other means also. NVC can be communicated through gestures and touch (Haptic communication), by body language or posture, by facial expression and eye contact. |
| Nonverbal communication | Nonverbal communication is usually understood as the process of communication through sending and receiving wordless (mostly visual) messages between people. Messages can be communicated through gestures and touch, by body language or posture, by facial expression and eye contact. Nonverbal messages could also be communicated through material exponential; meaning, objects or artifacts(such as clothing, hairstyles or architecture). |
| Online | The terms online and offline (also on-line and off-line) have specific meanings with respect to computer technology and telecommunication. In general, 'online' indicates a state of connectivity, while 'offline' indicates a disconnected state. In common usage, 'online' often refers to the Internet or the World Wide Web. |
| Femininity | Femininity is a set of attributes, behaviors, and roles generally associated with girls and women. Though socially constructed, femininity is made up of both socially defined and biologically created factors. This makes it distinct from the simple definition of the biological female sex, as women, men, and transgender people can all exhibit feminine traits. |
| Gender role | Gender roles refer to the set of social and behavioral norms that are considered to be socially appropriate for individuals of a specific sex in the context of a specific culture, which differ widely between cultures and over time. |

# Chapter 2. Culture and Gender

CHAPTER HIGHLIGHTS & NOTES: KEY TERMS, PEOPLE, PLACES, CONCEPTS

|  |  |
|---|---|
|  | There are differences of opinion as to whether observed gender differences in behavior and personality characteristics are, at least in part, due to cultural or social factors, and therefore, the product of socialization experiences, or to what extent gender differences are due to biological and physiological differences. |
|  | Views on gender-based differentiation in the workplace and in interpersonal relationships have often undergone profound changes as a result of feminist and/or economic influences, but there are still considerable differences in gender roles in almost all societies. |
| Metrosexual | Metrosexual is a neologism derived from metropolitan and heterosexual coined in 1994 describing a man (especially one living in an urban, post-industrial, capitalist culture) who spends a lot of time and money on shopping for his appearance. |
| FINANCIAL | FINANCIAL is the weekly English-language newspaper with offices in Tbilisi, Georgia and Kiev, Ukraine. Published by Intelligence Group LLC, FINANCIAL is focused on opinion leaders and top business decision-makers; It's about world's largest companies, investing, careers, and small business. It is distributed in Georgia and Ukraine. |
| Heterosexuality | Heterosexuality is romantic or sexual attraction or behavior between persons of opposite sex or gender in the gender binary. As a sexual orientation, heterosexuality refers to 'an enduring pattern of or disposition to experience sexual, affectional, physical or romantic attractions to persons of the opposite sex'; it also refers to 'an individual's sense of personal and social identity based on those attractions, behaviors expressing them, and membership in a community of others who share them'. The term is usually applied to human beings, but it is also observed in all mammals. |
| Intersex | Intersex, in humans and other animals, is the presence of intermediate or atypical combinations of physical features that usually distinguish female from male. This is usually understood to be congenital, involving chromosomal, morphologic, genital and/or gonadal anomalies, such as diversion from typical XX-female or XY-male presentations, e.g., sex reversal (XY-female, XX-male), genital ambiguity, or sex developmental differences. An intersex individual may have biological characteristics of both the male and the female sexes. |
| Sexual attraction | Sexual attraction is attraction on the basis of sexual desire or the quality of arousing such interest. Sexual attractiveness or sex appeal refers to an individual's ability to attract the sexual or erotic interest of another person, and is a factor in sexual selection or mate choice. The attraction can be to the physical or other qualities or traits of a person, or to such qualities in the context in which they appear. |
| Prevention | Prevention refers to: |

## Chapter 2. Culture and Gender

CHAPTER HIGHLIGHTS & NOTES: KEY TERMS, PEOPLE, PLACES, CONCEPTS

| | |
|---|---|
| | · Preventive medicine · Hazard Prevention, the process of risk study and elimination and mitigation in emergency management · Risk Prevention · Risk management · Preventive maintenance · Crime Prevention |
| | · Prevention, an album by Scottish band De Rosa · Prevention a magazine about health in the United States · Prevent (company), a textile company from Slovenia · Prevent (campaign), an anti-radicalization program in the United Kingdom |
| Asexuality | Asexuality in its broadest sense, describes lack of sexual attraction, or interest in or desire for sex. Sometimes, it is considered a lack of a sexual orientation. One commonly cited study placed the incidence rate of asexuality at 1%. |
| Linguistic | Linguistic s is the scientific study of language. Someone who engages in this study is called a linguist. Linguistic s can be theoretical or applied. |

CHAPTER QUIZ: KEY TERMS, PEOPLE, PLACES, CONCEPTS

1. _____ is usually understood as the process of communication through sending and receiving wordless (mostly visual) messages between people. Messages can be communicated through gestures and touch, by body language or posture, by facial expression and eye contact. Nonverbal messages could also be communicated through material exponential; meaning, objects or artifacts(such as clothing, hairstyles or architecture).

   a. Paralanguage
   b. Nonverbal communication
   c. Reply
   d. Sigh

2. _____ occurs when a suspicious observer discounts cues of truthfulness, given the observer's need to conform his/her observations of suspicions of deception. Essentially _____ occurs 'when the lie catcher fails to consider that a truthful person who is under stress may appear to be lying.' (Ekman, 1985).

   The term relates to the Shakespeare play in which Othello misinterprets Desdemona's reaction to Cassio's death.

   a. Out-group homogeneity
   b. Overjustification effect
   c. SpoCon
   d. Othello error

## Chapter 2. Culture and Gender

CHAPTER QUIZ: KEY TERMS, PEOPLE, PLACES, CONCEPTS

3. In semantics, a modifier is said to be _____ (or defining) if it restricts the reference of its head. For example, in 'the red car is fancier than the blue one', red and blue are _____, because they restrict which cars car and one are referring to. ('The car is fancier than the one' would make little sense).

    a. Restrictive
    b. Band-pass filter
    c. Bar joke
    d. Barbara Bauer Literary Agency

4. _____s are sentences or concepts with practical, i. e. action-oriented (rather than descriptive, explanatory, or expressive) import. _____s imply 'ought'-type statements or assertions, in distinction to descriptions which provide 'is'-type statements or assertions. Some common sentences that are _____s include commands, permissions, and prohibitions.

    a. Norm
    b. Performative utterance
    c. Port-Royal Grammar
    d. Principle of compositionality

5. _____ is a neologism derived from metropolitan and heterosexual coined in 1994 describing a man (especially one living in an urban, post-industrial, capitalist culture) who spends a lot of time and money on shopping for his appearance.

    a. Motorway man
    b. Nerd
    c. New Russian
    d. Metrosexual

**ANSWER KEY**
**Chapter 2. Culture and Gender**

1. b
2. d
3. a
4. a
5. d

## You can take the complete Chapter Practice Test

**for Chapter 2. Culture and Gender**
on all key terms, persons, places, and concepts.

## Online 99 Cents

### http://www.epub21.1.20820.2.cram101.com/

Use www.Cram101.com for all your study needs

including Cram101's online interactive problem solving labs in

chemistry, statistics, mathematics, and more.

# Chapter 3. Communication and the Self

CHAPTER OUTLINE: KEY TERMS, PEOPLE, PLACES, CONCEPTS

| FINANCIAL |
| Personal network |
| Gender role |
| Prevention |
| Autism |
| Self-fulfilling prophecy |
| Internet |
| Communication |
| Crocker |
| Spelling bee |
| Affection |
| Inclusion |
| Procedural |
| Franking |
| Autonomy |
| Social penetration theory |
| Online |
| Nonverbal communication |
| Norm |

# Chapter 3. Communication and the Self
CHAPTER OUTLINE: KEY TERMS, PEOPLE, PLACES, CONCEPTS

| | Norm of reciprocity |
| | Reciprocity |
| | Sexual attraction |
| | Direct marketing |

CHAPTER HIGHLIGHTS & NOTES: KEY TERMS, PEOPLE, PLACES, CONCEPTS

| | |
|---|---|
| FINANCIAL | FINANCIAL is the weekly English-language newspaper with offices in Tbilisi, Georgia and Kiev, Ukraine. Published by Intelligence Group LLC, FINANCIAL is focused on opinion leaders and top business decision-makers; It's about world's largest companies, investing, careers, and small business. It is distributed in Georgia and Ukraine. |
| Personal network | A personal network is a set of human contacts known to an individual, with whom that individual would expect to interact at intervals to support a given set of activities.<br><br>Personal networks are intended to be mutually beneficial--extending the concept of teamwork beyond the immediate peer group. The term is usually encountered in the workplace, though it could apply equally to other pursuits outside work. |
| Gender role | Gender roles refer to the set of social and behavioral norms that are considered to be socially appropriate for individuals of a specific sex in the context of a specific culture, which differ widely between cultures and over time. There are differences of opinion as to whether observed gender differences in behavior and personality characteristics are, at least in part, due to cultural or social factors, and therefore, the product of socialization experiences, or to what extent gender differences are due to biological and physiological differences.<br><br>Views on gender-based differentiation in the workplace and in interpersonal relationships have often undergone profound changes as a result of feminist and/or economic influences, but there are still considerable differences in gender roles in almost all societies. |
| Prevention | Prevention refers to: |

# Chapter 3. Communication and the Self

CHAPTER HIGHLIGHTS & NOTES: KEY TERMS, PEOPLE, PLACES, CONCEPTS

· Preventive medicine · Hazard Prevention, the process of risk study and elimination and mitigation in emergency management · Risk Prevention · Risk management · Preventive maintenance · Crime Prevention

· Prevention, an album by Scottish band De Rosa · Prevention a magazine about health in the United States · Prevent (company), a textile company from Slovenia · Prevent (campaign), an anti-radicalization program in the United Kingdom

| | |
|---|---|
| Autism | Autism is a disorder of neural development characterized by impaired social interaction and communication, and by restricted and repetitive behavior. For a diagnosis to be made, symptoms must become apparent before a child is three years old. Autism affects information processing in the brain by altering how nerve cells and their synapses connect and organize; how this occurs is not well understood. |
| Self-fulfilling prophecy | A self-fulfilling prophecy is a prediction that directly or indirectly causes itself to become true, by the very terms of the prophecy itself, due to positive feedback between belief and behavior. Although examples of such prophecies can be found in literature as far back as ancient Greece and ancient India, it is 20th-century sociologist Robert K. Merton who is credited with coining the expression 'self-fulfilling prophecy' and formalizing its structure and consequences. In his book Social Theory and Social Structure, Merton defines self-fulfilling prophecy in the following terms: e.g. when Roxanna falsely believes her marriage will fail, her fears of such failure actually cause the marriage to fail. |
| Internet | The Internet is a global system of interconnected computer networks that use the standard Internet Protocol Suite (TCP/IP) to serve billions of users worldwide. It is a network of networks that consists of millions of private, public, academic, business, and government networks, of local to global scope, that are linked by a broad array of electronic, wireless and optical networking technologies. The Internet carries a vast range of information resources and services, such as the inter-linked hypertext documents of the World Wide Web (WWW) and the infrastructure to support electronic mail. |
| Communication | Communication is the activity of conveying information. Communication has been derived from the Latin word 'communis', meaning to share. Communication requires a sender, a message, and an intended recipient, although the receiver need not be present or aware of the sender's intent to communicate at the time of communication; thus communication can occur across vast distances in time and space. |
| Crocker | Crocker is a team sport played between two large teams. Its origins are in cricket and baseball. It also makes the use of a soccer ball which may explain its name. |

# Chapter 3. Communication and the Self

CHAPTER HIGHLIGHTS & NOTES: KEY TERMS, PEOPLE, PLACES, CONCEPTS

| | |
|---|---|
| Spelling bee | A spelling bee is a competition where contestants, usually children, are asked to spell English words. The concept is thought to have originated in the United States. Today, National Spelling Bee competitions for English are held in the United States, United Kingdom, Australia, New Zealand, Canada, Indonesia and India among others. |
| Affection | In Celtic linguistics, affection (so known as vowel affection or infection) is the change in the quity of a vowel under the influence of the vowel of the following, fin syllable. The vowel triggering the change may or may not still be present in the modern language.<br><br>The two main types of affection are a-infection and i-infection. |
| Inclusion | Miller and Katz (2002) presents a common definition of an inclusive value system where they say, 'Inclusion is a sense of belonging: feeling respected, valued for who you are; feeling a level of supportive energy and commitment from others so than you can do your best work.' Inclusion is a shift in organization culture. The process of inclusion engages each individual and makes people feeling valued essential to the success of the organization. Individuals function at full capacity, feel more valued, and included in the organization's mission. |
| Procedural | A Procedural is a cross-genre type of literature, film, or television program involving a sequence of technical detail. A documentary film may be written in a procedural style to heighten narrative interest.<br><br>Types<br><br>Television<br><br>Fiction<br><br>In television, 'procedural' specifically refers to a genre of programs in which a problem is introduced, investigated and solved all within the same episode. |
| Franking | Franking are any and all devices or markings such as postage stamps (including printed and/or embossed on postal stationery), printed or stamped impressions, codings, labels, manuscript writings (including 'privilege' signatures), and/or any other authorized form of markings affixed or applied to mails to qualify them to be postally serviced. An 1832 stampless single-sheet 'Liverpool Ship Letter' pen franked 'Paid 5' by a U.S. postal clerk in Philadelphia, PA<br><br>While all affixed postage stamps and other markings applied to mail to qualify it for postal service are Franking (or 'franks'), not all types and methods are used to frank all types or classes of mails. |

# Chapter 3. Communication and the Self

CHAPTER HIGHLIGHTS & NOTES: KEY TERMS, PEOPLE, PLACES, CONCEPTS

| | |
|---|---|
| Autonomy | Autonomy is a concept found in moral, political, and bioethical philosophy. Within these contexts, it refers to the capacity of a rational individual to make an informed, un-coerced decision. In moral and political philosophy, autonomy is often used as the basis for determining moral responsibility for one's actions. |
| Social penetration theory | Social Penetration Theory states that as relationships develop, communication moves from relatively shallow, non-intimate levels to deeper, more personal ones.<br><br>The theory was formulated by psychology professors Irwin Altman and Dalmas Taylor as their attempt to describe the dynamics of relational closeness.<br><br>They proposed that closeness occurs through a gradual process of self-disclosure, and closeness develops if the participants proceed in a gradual and orderly fashion from superficial to intimate levels of exchange as a function of both immediate and forecast outcomes. |
| Online | The terms online and offline (also on-line and off-line) have specific meanings with respect to computer technology and telecommunication. In general, 'online' indicates a state of connectivity, while 'offline' indicates a disconnected state. In common usage, 'online' often refers to the Internet or the World Wide Web. |
| Nonverbal communication | Nonverbal communication is usually understood as the process of communication through sending and receiving wordless (mostly visual) messages between people. Messages can be communicated through gestures and touch, by body language or posture, by facial expression and eye contact. Nonverbal messages could also be communicated through material exponential; meaning, objects or artifacts(such as clothing, hairstyles or architecture). |
| Norm | Norms are sentences or concepts with practical, i. e. action-oriented (rather than descriptive, explanatory, or expressive) import. Norms imply 'ought'-type statements or assertions, in distinction to descriptions which provide 'is'-type statements or assertions. Some common sentences that are norms include commands, permissions, and prohibitions. |
| Norm of reciprocity | The Norm of reciprocity is the social expectation that people will respond to each other in kind-- returning benefits for benefits, and responding with either indifference or hostility to harms. The social Norm of reciprocity often takes different forms in different areas of social life, or in different societies. All of them, however, are distinct from related ideas such as gratitude, the Golden Rule, or mutual goodwill. |
| Reciprocity | Theoretical efforts have been made to study the nontrivial properties of complex networks, such as clustering, scale-free degree distribution, community structures, etc. Here Reciprocity is another quantity to specifically characterize directed networks. |

# Chapter 3. Communication and the Self

## CHAPTER HIGHLIGHTS & NOTES: KEY TERMS, PEOPLE, PLACES, CONCEPTS

| | |
|---|---|
| Sexual attraction | Sexual attraction is attraction on the basis of sexual desire or the quality of arousing such interest. Sexual attractiveness or sex appeal refers to an individual's ability to attract the sexual or erotic interest of another person, and is a factor in sexual selection or mate choice. The attraction can be to the physical or other qualities or traits of a person, or to such qualities in the context in which they appear. |
| Direct marketing | Direct marketing is a form of advertising that reaches its audience without using traditional formal channels of advertising, such as TV, newspapers or radio. Businesses communicate straight to the consumer with advertising techniques such as fliers, catalogue distribution, promotional letters, and street advertising.<br><br>Direct Advertising is a sub-discipline and type of marketing. |

## CHAPTER QUIZ: KEY TERMS, PEOPLE, PLACES, CONCEPTS

1. _____ states that as relationships develop, communication moves from relatively shallow, non-intimate levels to deeper, more personal ones.

   The theory was formulated by psychology professors Irwin Altman and Dalmas Taylor as their attempt to describe the dynamics of relational closeness.

   They proposed that closeness occurs through a gradual process of self-disclosure, and closeness develops if the participants proceed in a gradual and orderly fashion from superficial to intimate levels of exchange as a function of both immediate and forecast outcomes.

   a. Uncertainty reduction theory
   b. Social penetration theory
   c. Psychological novel
   d. Psychological thriller

2. . _____ are any and all devices or markings such as postage stamps (including printed and/or embossed on postal stationery), printed or stamped impressions, codings, labels, manuscript writings (including 'privilege' signatures), and/or any other authorized form of markings affixed or applied to mails to qualify them to be postally serviced. An 1832 stampless single-sheet 'Liverpool Ship Letter' pen franked 'Paid 5' by a U.S. postal clerk in Philadelphia, PA

   While all affixed postage stamps and other markings applied to mail to qualify it for postal service are _____ (or 'franks'), not all types and methods are used to frank all types or classes of mails. Each of the world's national postal administrations establish and regulate the specific methods and standards of _____ as they apply to domestic operations within their own postal systems.

## Chapter 3. Communication and the Self

CHAPTER QUIZ: KEY TERMS, PEOPLE, PLACES, CONCEPTS

a. Baka
b. Prosimetrum
c. Franking
d. Psychological thriller

3. The terms _____ and offline (also on-line and off-line) have specific meanings with respect to computer technology and telecommunication. In general, '_____' indicates a state of connectivity, while 'offline' indicates a disconnected state. In common usage, '_____' often refers to the Internet or the World Wide Web.

    a. Online
    b. Interweb
    c. IANAL
    d. Egoboo

4. _____ is the weekly English-language newspaper with offices in Tbilisi, Georgia and Kiev, Ukraine. Published by Intelligence Group LLC, _____ is focused on opinion leaders and top business decision-makers; It's about world's largest companies, investing, careers, and small business. It is distributed in Georgia and Ukraine.

    a. Baka
    b. Band-pass filter
    c. Bar joke
    d. FINANCIAL

5. _____ refers to:

    · Preventive medicine · Hazard _____, the process of risk study and elimination and mitigation in emergency management · Risk _____ · Risk management · Preventive maintenance · Crime _____

    · _____, an album by Scottish band De Rosa · _____ a magazine about health in the United States · Prevent (company), a textile company from Slovenia · Prevent (campaign), an anti-radicalization program in the United Kingdom

    a. Federation for American Immigration Reform
    b. Strong verb
    c. Weak
    d. Prevention

## ANSWER KEY
### Chapter 3. Communication and the Self

1. b
2. c
3. a
4. d
5. d

## You can take the complete Chapter Practice Test

### for Chapter 3. Communication and the Self
on all key terms, persons, places, and concepts.

### Online 99 Cents

### http://www.epub21.1.20820.3.cram101.com/

Use www.Cram101.com for all your study needs

including Cram101's online interactive problem solving labs in

chemistry, statistics, mathematics, and more.

# Chapter 4. Interpersonal Perception

CHAPTER OUTLINE: KEY TERMS, PEOPLE, PLACES, CONCEPTS

- Interpersonal perception
- Procedural
- Organizations
- Autonomy
- AVATAR
- Social network
- Personal network
- Spelling bee
- Negativity bias
- Self-serving bias
- Othello error
- Direct marketing

# Chapter 4. Interpersonal Perception

CHAPTER HIGHLIGHTS & NOTES: KEY TERMS, PEOPLE, PLACES, CONCEPTS

| | |
|---|---|
| Interpersonal perception | Interpersonal perception is an area of research in social psychology which examines the beliefs that interacting people have about each other. This area differs from social cognition and person perception by being interpersonal rather than intrapersonal, and thus requiring the interaction of at least two actual people. •accuracy - the correctness of A's beliefs about B•self-other agreement - whether A's beliefs about B matches B's beliefs about himself•similarity - whether A's and B's beliefs match•projection/assumed similarity - whether A's beliefs about B match A's beliefs about herself•recrocity - the similarity of A's and B's beliefs about each other•meta-accuracy - whether A knows how others see her•assumed projection - whether A thinks others see her as she sees them<br><br>These variables cannot be assessed in studies that ask people to form beliefs about fictitious targets. |
| Procedural | A Procedural is a cross-genre type of literature, film, or television program involving a sequence of technical detail. A documentary film may be written in a procedural style to heighten narrative interest.<br><br>Types<br><br>Television<br><br>Fiction<br><br>In television, 'procedural' specifically refers to a genre of programs in which a problem is introduced, investigated and solved all within the same episode. |
| Organizations | Organizations<br><br>· ALLARM · National Coalition on Racism in Sports and Media · STAR · Honor Indians Institute<br><br>Articles<br><br>· 'Crimes Against Humanity' by Ward Churchill<br><br>Parody<br><br>· Turning the Tables on Racist Mascots · Alternative Indian Mascots |
| Autonomy | Autonomy is a concept found in moral, political, and bioethical philosophy. Within these contexts, it refers to the capacity of a rational individual to make an informed, un-coerced decision. |

# Chapter 4. Interpersonal Perception

CHAPTER HIGHLIGHTS & NOTES: KEY TERMS, PEOPLE, PLACES, CONCEPTS

| | |
|---|---|
| AVATAR | The AVATAR protocol (AVATAR Recreator) is a system of escape sequences occasionally used on Bulletin Board Systems (BBSes). It has largely the same functionality as the more popular ANSI escape codes, but has the advantage that the escape sequences are much shorter. AVATAR can thus render colored text and artwork much faster over slow connections. |
| Social network | A social network is a social structure made up of a set of actors (such as individuals or organizations) and the dyadic ties between these actors (such as relationships, connections, or interactions). A social network perspective is employed to model the structure of a social group, how this structure influences other variables, or how structures change over time. The study of these structures uses methods in social network analysis to identify influential nodes, local and global structures, and network dynamics. |
| Personal network | A personal network is a set of human contacts known to an individual, with whom that individual would expect to interact at intervals to support a given set of activities.<br><br>Personal networks are intended to be mutually beneficial--extending the concept of teamwork beyond the immediate peer group. The term is usually encountered in the workplace, though it could apply equally to other pursuits outside work. |
| Spelling bee | A spelling bee is a competition where contestants, usually children, are asked to spell English words. The concept is thought to have originated in the United States. Today, National Spelling Bee competitions for English are held in the United States, United Kingdom, Australia, New Zealand, Canada, Indonesia and India among others. |
| Negativity bias | Negativity bias is the name for a psychological phenomenon by which humans pay more attention to and give more weight to negative rather than positive experiences or other kinds of information. This shows up in a number of domains, including:•When given a piece of positive information and a piece of negative information about a stranger, people's judgment of the stranger will be negative, rather than neutral (assuming the two pieces of information are not severely imbalanced).•If a person has a good experience and a bad experience close together, they will feel worse than neutral. This is true even if they would independently judge the two experiences to be of similar magnitude.•Negative information in the simple form of negation has greater impact and creates more attention than similar positive information in the form of affirmation. |
| Self-serving bias | A self-serving bias occurs when people attribute their successes to internal or personal factors but attribute their failures to situational factors beyond their control. The self-serving bias can be seen in the common human tendency to take credit for success but to deny responsibility for failure.. |

# Chapter 4. Interpersonal Perception

CHAPTER HIGHLIGHTS & NOTES: KEY TERMS, PEOPLE, PLACES, CONCEPTS

| | |
|---|---|
| Othello error | Othello error occurs when a suspicious observer discounts cues of truthfulness, given the observer's need to conform his/her observations of suspicions of deception. Essentially Othello error occurs 'when the lie catcher fails to consider that a truthful person who is under stress may appear to be lying.' (Ekman, 1985). <br><br> The term relates to the Shakespeare play in which Othello misinterprets Desdemona's reaction to Cassio's death. |
| Direct marketing | Direct marketing is a form of advertising that reaches its audience without using traditional formal channels of advertising, such as TV, newspapers or radio. Businesses communicate straight to the consumer with advertising techniques such as fliers, catalogue distribution, promotional letters, and street advertising. <br><br> Direct Advertising is a sub-discipline and type of marketing. |

CHAPTER QUIZ: KEY TERMS, PEOPLE, PLACES, CONCEPTS

1. _____ is an area of research in social psychology which examines the beliefs that interacting people have about each other. This area differs from social cognition and person perception by being interpersonal rather than intrapersonal, and thus requiring the interaction of at least two actual people. •accuracy - the correctness of A's beliefs about B•self-other agreement - whether A's beliefs about B matches B's beliefs about himself•similarity - whether A's and B's beliefs match•projection/assumed similarity - whether A's beliefs about B match A's beliefs about herself•recrocity - the similarity of A's and B's beliefs about each other•meta-accuracy - whether A knows how others see her•assumed projection - whether A thinks others see her as she sees them

These variables cannot be assessed in studies that ask people to form beliefs about fictitious targets.

a. Acculturation
b. Achievement ideology
c. Interpersonal perception
d. Alloplastic adaptation

2. . _____ is a concept found in moral, political, and bioethical philosophy. Within these contexts, it refers to the capacity of a rational individual to make an informed, un-coerced decision. In moral and political philosophy, _____ is often used as the basis for determining moral responsibility for one's actions.

a. ad Herennium
b. Prosimetrum

# Chapter 4. Interpersonal Perception

CHAPTER QUIZ: KEY TERMS, PEOPLE, PLACES, CONCEPTS

c. Psychological novel
d. Autonomy

3. _____ is a form of advertising that reaches its audience without using traditional formal channels of advertising, such as TV, newspapers or radio. Businesses communicate straight to the consumer with advertising techniques such as fliers, catalogue distribution, promotional letters, and street advertising.

Direct Advertising is a sub-discipline and type of marketing.

a. Database marketing
b. Relationship marketing
c. Direct marketing
d. Trait ascription bias

4. A _____ is a cross-genre type of literature, film, or television program involving a sequence of technical detail. A documentary film may be written in a _____ style to heighten narrative interest.

Types

Television

Fiction

In television, '_____' specifically refers to a genre of programs in which a problem is introduced, investigated and solved all within the same episode.

a. Prose poetry
b. Prosimetrum
c. Procedural
d. Psychological thriller

5. The _____ protocol (_____ Recreator) is a system of escape sequences occasionally used on Bulletin Board Systems (BBSes). It has largely the same functionality as the more popular ANSI escape codes, but has the advantage that the escape sequences are much shorter. _____ can thus render colored text and artwork much faster over slow connections.

a. ad Herennium
b. AVATAR
c. Psychological novel
d. Psychological thriller

**ANSWER KEY**
Chapter 4. Interpersonal Perception

1. c
2. d
3. c
4. c
5. b

## You can take the complete Chapter Practice Test

### for Chapter 4. Interpersonal Perception
on all key terms, persons, places, and concepts.

### Online 99 Cents

### http://www.epub21.1.20820.4.cram101.com/

Use www.Cram101.com for all your study needs

including Cram101's online interactive problem solving labs in

chemistry, statistics, mathematics, and more.

# Chapter 5. Language

CHAPTER OUTLINE: KEY TERMS, PEOPLE, PLACES, CONCEPTS

- Abstraction
- Onomatopoeia
- Phonological rule
- Semantics
- Loaded language
- Sapir-Whorf hypothesis
- Linguistic determinism
- Linguistic relativity
- Aristotle
- Personal network
- Persuasion
- Etho
- Pathos
- Communication
- Communication accommodation theory
- Credibility
- Berber languages
- Equivocation
- FINANCIAL

## Chapter 5. Language
CHAPTER OUTLINE: KEY TERMS, PEOPLE, PLACES, CONCEPTS

- Interpersonal communication
- Nonverbal
- Nonverbal communication
- Online
- Blog
- Affection
- Weasel word
- Euphemism
- Direct marketing
- Doublespeak
- Intrapersonal communication
- Defamation
- Hate speech
- Profanity
- Gender role
- Sexual attraction
- Opinion
- I-statement
- Speech

# Chapter 5. Language

CHAPTER HIGHLIGHTS & NOTES: KEY TERMS, PEOPLE, PLACES, CONCEPTS

| | |
|---|---|
| Abstraction | Abstraction is a process by which higher concepts are derived from the usage and classification of literal ('real' or 'concrete') concepts, first principles, or other methods. 'An abstraction' is the product of this process - a concept that acts as a super-categorical noun for all subordinate concepts, and connects any related concepts as a group, field, or category.<br><br>Abstractions may be formed by reducing the information content of a concept or an observable phenomenon, typically to retain only information which is relevant for a particular purpose. |
| Onomatopoeia | An Onomatopoeia or onomatopŃ"ia, from the Greek á½€νοματοποιĺ¯α , is a word that imitates or suggests the source of the sound that it describes. Onomatopoeia refers to the property of such words. Common occurrences of Onomatopoeias include animal noises, such as 'oink' or 'meow' or 'roar'. |
| Phonological rule | A phonological rule is a formal way of exessing a systematic phonological or morphophonological ocess or diachronic sound change in language. Phonological rules are commonly used in generative phonology as a notation to capture sound-related operations and computations the human brain performs when oducing or comehending spoken language. They may use phonetic notation or distinctive features or both. |
| Semantics | Semantics is the study of meaning. It typically focuses on the relation between signifiers, such as words, phrases, signs and symbols, and what they stand for, their denotata.<br><br>Linguistic semantics is the study of meaning that is used by humans to express themselves through language. |
| Loaded language | In rhetoric, loaded language is wording that attempts to influence the certain audience by using an appeal to emotion.<br><br>Loaded words and phrases have strong emotional implications and involve strongly positive or negative reactions beyond their literal meaning. For example, the phrase tax relief refers literay to changes that reduce the amount of tax citizens must pay. |
| Sapir-Whorf hypothesis | The linguistic relativity principle (also known as the Sapir-Whorf hypothesis) is the idea that the varying cultural concepts and categories inherent in different languages affect the cognitive classification of the experienced world in such a way that speakers of different languages think and behave differently because of it.<br><br>The idea that linguistic structure influences the cognition of language users has bearings on the fields of anthropological linguistics, psychology, psycholinguistics, neurolinguistics, cognitive science, linguistic anthropology, sociology of language and philosophy of language, and it has been the subject of extensive studies in all of these fields. |

# Chapter 5. Language

**CHAPTER HIGHLIGHTS & NOTES: KEY TERMS, PEOPLE, PLACES, CONCEPTS**

| | |
|---|---|
| Linguistic determinism | Linguistic determinism is the idea that language and its structures limit and determine human knowledge or thought. Determinism itself refers to the viewpoint that all events are caused by previous events, and linguistic determinism can be used broadly to refer to a number of specific views. |
| | For example, those who follow analytic philosophy from Ludwig Wittgenstein onward might accept the proposition that, as Wittgenstein said in the Tractatus Logico-Philosophicus, 'The limits of my language mean the limits of my wor.' (proposition 5.6), 'The subject does not belong to the wor, but it is a limit of the wor.' (proposition 5.632) and 'About what one can not speak, one must remain silent.' (proposition 7). |
| Linguistic relativity | The principle of linguistic relativity holds that the structure of a language affects the ways in which its speakers are able to conceptualize their world, i.e. their world view. Popularly known as the Sapir-Whorf hypothesis, or Whorfianism, the principle is often defined as having two versions: (i) the strong version that language determines thought and that linguistic categories limit and determine cognitive categories and (ii) the weak version that linguistic categories and usage influence thought and certain kinds of non-linguistic behavior. |
| | The idea was first clearly expressed by 19th century thinkers, such as Wilhelm von Humboldt, who saw language as the expression of the spirit of a nation. |
| Aristotle | Aristotle was a Greek philosopher, a student of Plato and teacher of Alexander the Great. His writings cover many subjects, including physics, metaphysics, poetry, theater, music, logic, rhetoric, linguistics, politics, government, ethics, biology, and zoology. Together with Plato and Socrates (Plato's teacher), Aristotle is one of the most important founding figures in Western philosophy. |
| Personal network | A personal network is a set of human contacts known to an individual, with whom that individual would expect to interact at intervals to support a given set of activities. |
| | Personal networks are intended to be mutually beneficial--extending the concept of teamwork beyond the immediate peer group. The term is usually encountered in the workplace, though it could apply equally to other pursuits outside work. |
| Persuasion | Persuasion is a form of social influence. It is the process of guiding people and oneself toward the adoption of an idea, attitude, or action by rational and symbolic (though not always logical) means. |
| | Persuasion methods are also sometimes referred to as Persuasion tactics strategies. |
| | According to Robert Cialdini in his book on Persuasion, he defined six 'weapons of influence': |

# Chapter 5. Language

CHAPTER HIGHLIGHTS & NOTES: KEY TERMS, PEOPLE, PLACES, CONCEPTS

| | |
|---|---|
| | · Reciprocity - People tend to return a favor. |
| Etho | Ethos , ethea (á¼¤θεα)) is a Greek word originally meaning 'accustomed place' , 'custom, habit', equivalent to Latin mores.

Ethos forms the root of ethikos (á¼ θικÏŒς), meaning 'moral, showing moral character'. To the Greeks ancient and modern, the meaning is simply 'the state of being', the inner source, the soul, the mind, and the original essence, that shapes and forms a person or animal. |
| Pathos | Pathos represents an appeal to the audience's emotions. Pathos is a communication technique used most often in rhetoric (where it is considered one of the three modes of persuasion, alongside ethos and logos), and in literature, film and other narrative art.

Emotional appeal can be accomplished in a multitude of ways:•by a metaphor or story telling, common as a hook,•by a general passion in the delivery and an overall emotion and sympathies of the speech or writing as determined by the audience. |
| Communication | Communication is the activity of conveying information. Communication has been derived from the Latin word 'communis', meaning to share. Communication requires a sender, a message, and an intended recipient, although the receiver need not be present or aware of the sender's intent to communicate at the time of communication; thus communication can occur across vast distances in time and space. |
| Communication accommodation theory | Communication accommodation theory is a theory of communication developed by Howard Giles. It argues that 'when people interact they adjust their speech, their vocal patterns and their gestures, to accommodate to others'. It explores the various reasons why individuals emphasize or minimize the social differences between themselves and their interlocutors through verbal and non-verbal communication. |
| Credibility | Credibility refers to the objective and subjective components of the believability of a source or message.

Traditionally, Credibility has two key components: trustworthiness and expertise, which both have objective and subjective components. Trustworthiness is based more on subjective factors, but can include objective measurements such as established reliability. |
| Berber languages | The Berber languages are a group of very closely related languages and dialects spoken in Morocco, Algeria, Tunisia, Libya, and the Egyptian area of Siwa, as well as by large Berber communities in parts of Niger and Mali. A relatively sparse but very old population extends into the whole Sahara and the northern part of the Sahel. |

# Chapter 5. Language

CHAPTER HIGHLIGHTS & NOTES: KEY TERMS, PEOPLE, PLACES, CONCEPTS

| | |
|---|---|
| Equivocation | Equivocation is classified as both a formal and informal fallacy. It is the misleading use of a term with more than one meaning or sense. |
| | It is often confused with amphiboly; however, Equivocation is ambiguity arising from the misleading use of a word and amphiboly is ambiguity arising from misleading use of punctuation or syntax. |
| FINANCIAL | FINANCIAL is the weekly English-language newspaper with offices in Tbilisi, Georgia and Kiev, Ukraine. Published by Intelligence Group LLC, FINANCIAL is focused on opinion leaders and top business decision-makers; It's about world's largest companies, investing, careers, and small business. It is distributed in Georgia and Ukraine. |
| Interpersonal communication | Interpersonal communication is usually defined by communication scholars in numerous ways, usually describing participants who are dependent upon one another. It can involve one on one conversations or individuals interacting with many people within a society. It helps us understand how and why people behave and communicate in different ways to construct and negotiate a social reality. |
| Nonverbal | Nonverbal communications (NVC) is usually understood as the process of communication through sending and receiving wordless messages. i.e, language is not one source of communication, there are other means also. NVC can be communicated through gestures and touch (Haptic communication), by body language or posture, by facial expression and eye contact. |
| Nonverbal communication | Nonverbal communication is usually understood as the process of communication through sending and receiving wordless (mostly visual) messages between people. Messages can be communicated through gestures and touch, by body language or posture, by facial expression and eye contact. Nonverbal messages could also be communicated through material exponential; meaning, objects or artifacts(such as clothing, hairstyles or architecture). |
| Online | The terms online and offline (also on-line and off-line) have specific meanings with respect to computer technology and telecommunication. In general, 'online' indicates a state of connectivity, while 'offline' indicates a disconnected state. In common usage, 'online' often refers to the Internet or the World Wide Web. |
| Blog | A blog is a type of website or part of a website. Blogs are usually maintained by an individual with regular entries of commentary, descriptions of events, or other material such as graphics or video. Entries are commonly displayed in reverse-chronological order. |
| Affection | In Celtic linguistics, affection (so known as vowel affection or infection) is the change in the quity of a vowel under the influence of the vowel of the following, fin syllable. |

# Chapter 5. Language

CHAPTER HIGHLIGHTS & NOTES: KEY TERMS, PEOPLE, PLACES, CONCEPTS

| | |
|---|---|
| | The vowel triggering the change may or may not still be present in the modern language. |
| | The two main types of affection are a-infection and i-infection. |
| Weasel word | A weasel word is an informal term for words and phrases aimed at creating an impression that something specific and meaningful has been said, when in fact only a vague or ambiguous claim has been communicated. |
| | For example, an advertisement may use a weasel phrase such as 'up to 50% off on all products'; this is misleading because the audience is invited to imagine many items reduced by the proclaimed 50%, but the words taken literally mean only that no discount will exceed 50%, and in practice, the vendor is free not to reduce any prices and still remain faithful to the wording of the advertisement. |
| | In other cases, words with a particular subjective effect are chosen. |
| Euphemism | A euphemism is a generally harmless word, name, or phrase that substitutes an offensive or suggestive one. Some euphemisms intend to amuse, while others intend to give positive appearances to negative events or even mislead entirely. Euphemisms also often take the place of profanity. |
| Direct marketing | Direct marketing is a form of advertising that reaches its audience without using traditional formal channels of advertising, such as TV, newspapers or radio. Businesses communicate straight to the consumer with advertising techniques such as fliers, catalogue distribution, promotional letters, and street advertising. |
| | Direct Advertising is a sub-discipline and type of marketing. |
| Doublespeak | Doublespeak is language that deliberately disguises, distorts, or reverses the meaning of words. Doublespeak may take the form of euphemisms (e.g., 'downsizing' for layoffs,'servicing the target' for bombing ), making the truth less unpleasant, without denying its nature. It may also be deployed as intentional ambiguity, or reversal of meaning (for example, naming a state of war 'peace'). |
| Intrapersonal communication | Intrapersonal communication is language use or thought internal to the communicator. It can be useful to envision intrapersonal communication occurring in the mind of the individual in a model which contains a sender, receiver, and feedback loop. |

# Chapter 5. Language

**CHAPTER HIGHLIGHTS & NOTES: KEY TERMS, PEOPLE, PLACES, CONCEPTS**

| | |
|---|---|
| Defamation | Defamation--also called calumny, vilification, traducement, slander (for transitory statements), and libel (for written, broadcast, or otherwise published words)--is the communication of a statement that makes a claim, expressly stated or implied to be factual, that may give an individual, business, product, group, government, or nation a negative image. This can be also any disparaging statement made by one person about another, which is communicated or published, whether true or false, depending on legal state. In Common Law it is usually a requirement that this claim be false and that the publication is communicated to someone other than the person defamed (the claimant). |
| Hate speech | Hate speech is speech perceived to disparage a person or group of people based on their social or ethnic group, such as race, gender, age, ethnicity, nationality, religion, sexual orientation, gender identity, disability, language ability, ideology, social class, occupation, appearance (height, weight, skin color, etc)., mental capacity, and any other distinction that might be considered by some as a liability. The term covers written as well as oral communication and some forms of behaviors in a public setting. It is also sometimes called antilocution and is the first point on Allport's scale which measures prejudice in a society. |
| Profanity | Profanity, cursing, foul speech, and cussing, is a show of disrespect, a desecration or debasement of someone or something, or the act of expressing intense emotions. Profanity can take the form of words, expressions, gestures, or other social behaviors that are socially constructed or interpreted as insulting, rude, vulgar, obscene, obnoxious, foul, desecrating or other forms.<br><br>The original meaning of the adjective profane referred to items not belonging to the church, e.g., 'The fort is the oldest profane building in the town, but the local monastery is older, and is the oldest building,' or 'besides designing churches, he also designed many profane buildings'. |
| Gender role | Gender roles refer to the set of social and behavioral norms that are considered to be socially appropriate for individuals of a specific sex in the context of a specific culture, which differ widely between cultures and over time. There are differences of opinion as to whether observed gender differences in behavior and personality characteristics are, at least in part, due to cultural or social factors, and therefore, the product of socialization experiences, or to what extent gender differences are due to biological and physiological differences.<br><br>Views on gender-based differentiation in the workplace and in interpersonal relationships have often undergone profound changes as a result of feminist and/or economic influences, but there are still considerable differences in gender roles in almost all societies. |
| Sexual attraction | Sexual attraction is attraction on the basis of sexual desire or the quality of arousing such interest. Sexual attractiveness or sex appeal refers to an individual's ability to attract the sexual or erotic interest of another person, and is a factor in sexual selection or mate choice. |

# Chapter 5. Language

## CHAPTER HIGHLIGHTS & NOTES: KEY TERMS, PEOPLE, PLACES, CONCEPTS

| | |
|---|---|
| Opinion | In general, an opinion is a subjective belief, and is the result of emotion or interpretation of facts. An opinion may be supported by an argument, although people may draw opposing opinions from the same set of facts. Opinions rarely change without new arguments being presented. |
| I-statement | An I-statement is a statement that begins with the word 'I'. It is frequently used in an attempt to be assertive without putting the listener on the defensive. It can be used to take ownership for one's feelings rather than saying they are caused by the other person. |
| Speech | Speech is the vocalized form of human communication. It is based upon the syntactic combination of lexicals and names that are drawn from very large (usually to about 10,000 different words) vocabularies. Each spoken word is created out of the phonetic combination of a limited set of vowel and consonant speech sound units. |

## CHAPTER QUIZ: KEY TERMS, PEOPLE, PLACES, CONCEPTS

1. _____ is the activity of conveying information. _____ has been derived from the Latin word 'communis', meaning to share. _____ requires a sender, a message, and an intended recipient, although the receiver need not be present or aware of the sender's intent to communicate at the time of _____; thus _____ can occur across vast distances in time and space.

    a. Communication complexity
    b. Communication endpoint
    c. Communication
    d. Communication for social change

2. _____ is the weekly English-language newspaper with offices in Tbilisi, Georgia and Kiev, Ukraine. Published by Intelligence Group LLC, _____ is focused on opinion leaders and top business decision-makers; It's about world's largest companies, investing, careers, and small business. It is distributed in Georgia and Ukraine.

    a. FINANCIAL
    b. Band-pass filter
    c. Bar joke
    d. Moabite language

3. . _____, cursing, foul speech, and cussing, is a show of disrespect, a desecration or debasement of someone or something, or the act of expressing intense emotions. _____ can take the form of words, expressions, gestures, or other social behaviors that are socially constructed or interpreted as insulting, rude, vulgar, obscene, obnoxious, foul, desecrating or other forms.

## Chapter 5. Language

CHAPTER QUIZ: KEY TERMS, PEOPLE, PLACES, CONCEPTS

The original meaning of the adjective profane referred to items not belonging to the church, e.g., 'The fort is the oldest profane building in the town, but the local monastery is older, and is the oldest building,' or 'besides designing churches, he also designed many profane buildings'.

    a. Bugger
    b. Bullshit
    c. Profanity
    d. Cock tease

4. _____ was a Greek philosopher, a student of Plato and teacher of Alexander the Great. His writings cover many subjects, including physics, metaphysics, poetry, theater, music, logic, rhetoric, linguistics, politics, government, ethics, biology, and zoology. Together with Plato and Socrates (Plato's teacher), _____ is one of the most important founding figures in Western philosophy.

    a. Aristotle
    b. Hugh Blair
    c. Gregory G. Colomb
    d. Robert T. Craig

5. A _____ is a generally harmless word, name, or phrase that substitutes an offensive or suggestive one. Some _____s intend to amuse, while others intend to give positive appearances to negative events or even mislead entirely. _____s also often take the place of profanity.

    a. Ideograph
    b. Ideological repression
    c. Indoctrinate U
    d. Euphemism

**ANSWER KEY**
**Chapter 5. Language**

1. c
2. a
3. c
4. a
5. d

---

## You can take the complete Chapter Practice Test

### for Chapter 5. Language
on all key terms, persons, places, and concepts.

## Online 99 Cents

### http://www.epub21.1.20820.5.cram101.com/

Use www.Cram101.com for all your study needs

including Cram101's online interactive problem solving labs in

chemistry, statistics, mathematics, and more.

# Chapter 6. Nonverbal Communication

CHAPTER OUTLINE: KEY TERMS, PEOPLE, PLACES, CONCEPTS

| | Facial expression |
| | Nonverbal communication |
| | FINANCIAL |
| | Nonverbal |
| | Reality television |
| | Communication |
| | Eye contact |
| | Aristotle |
| | Status symbol |
| | Online |
| | Social network |
| | Psychoanalytic literary criticism |
| | Abstraction |
| | Emblem |
| | Kinesics |
| | ADHD |
| | Internet |
| | Prevention |
| | Direct marketing |

## Chapter 6. Nonverbal Communication
CHAPTER OUTLINE: KEY TERMS, PEOPLE, PLACES, CONCEPTS

- Enunciation
- Filler
- Inflection
- Pronunciation
- Speech
- Gender role
- Proxemics
- Sexual attraction
- Academies
- Halo effect
- Chronemics
- Clubflyer
- Autonomy
- Interpreting

# Chapter 6. Nonverbal Communication

CHAPTER HIGHLIGHTS & NOTES: KEY TERMS, PEOPLE, PLACES, CONCEPTS

| | |
|---|---|
| Facial expression | A Facial expression results from one or more motions or positions of the muscles of the face. These movements convey the emotional state of the individual to observers. Facial expressions are a form of nonverbal communication. |
| Nonverbal communication | Nonverbal communication is usually understood as the process of communication through sending and receiving wordless (mostly visual) messages between people. Messages can be communicated through gestures and touch, by body language or posture, by facial expression and eye contact. Nonverbal messages could also be communicated through material exponential; meaning, objects or artifacts(such as clothing, hairstyles or architecture). |
| FINANCIAL | FINANCIAL is the weekly English-language newspaper with offices in Tbilisi, Georgia and Kiev, Ukraine. Published by Intelligence Group LLC, FINANCIAL is focused on opinion leaders and top business decision-makers; It's about world's largest companies, investing, careers, and small business. It is distributed in Georgia and Ukraine. |
| Nonverbal | Nonverbal communications (NVC) is usually understood as the process of communication through sending and receiving wordless messages. i.e, language is not one source of communication, there are other means also. NVC can be communicated through gestures and touch (Haptic communication), by body language or posture, by facial expression and eye contact. |
| Reality television | · 'The Biggest Loser' 6,248 · 'American Idol,' 4,636 · 'Extreme Makeover: Home Edition,' 3,371 · 'America's Toughest Jobs,' 2,807 · 'One Tree Hill,' 2,575 · 'Deal or No Deal,' 2,292 · 'America's Next Top Model,' 2,241 · 'Last Comic Standing,' 1,993 · 'Kitchen Nightmares' 1,853 · 'Hell's Kitchen,' 1,807<br><br>Some commentators have said that the name 'Reality television' is an inaccurate description for several styles of program included in the genre. Irene McGee, a castmember on the 1998 The Real World Seattle, has done public speaking tours about the negative and misleading aspects of reality TV.<br><br>In competition-based programs such as Big Brother and Survivor, and other special living environment shows like The Real World, the producers design the format of the show and control the day-to-day activities and the environment, creating a completely fabricated world in which the competition plays out. Producers specifically select the participants and use carefully designed scenarios, challenges, events, and settings to encourage particular behaviors and conflicts. |
| Communication | Communication is the activity of conveying information. Communication has been derived from the Latin word 'communis', meaning to share. |

# Chapter 6. Nonverbal Communication

CHAPTER HIGHLIGHTS & NOTES: KEY TERMS, PEOPLE, PLACES, CONCEPTS

| | |
|---|---|
| Eye contact | Eye contact is a meeting of the eyes between two individuals. |
| | In human beings, eye contact is a form of nonverbal communication and is thought to have a large influence on social behavior. Coined in the early to mid-1960s, the term has come in the West to often define the act as a meaningful and important sign of confidence and social communication. |
| Aristotle | Aristotle was a Greek philosopher, a student of Plato and teacher of Alexander the Great. His writings cover many subjects, including physics, metaphysics, poetry, theater, music, logic, rhetoric, linguistics, politics, government, ethics, biology, and zoology. Together with Plato and Socrates (Plato's teacher), Aristotle is one of the most important founding figures in Western philosophy. |
| Status symbol | A status symbol is a perceived visible, external denotation of one's social position and perceived indicator of economic or social status. Many luxury goods are often considered status symbols. Status symbol is also a sociological term - as part of social and sociological symbolic interactionism - relating to how individuals and groups interact and interpret various cultural symbols. |
| Online | The terms online and offline (also on-line and off-line) have specific meanings with respect to computer technology and telecommunication. In general, 'online' indicates a state of connectivity, while 'offline' indicates a disconnected state. In common usage, 'online' often refers to the Internet or the World Wide Web. |
| Social network | A social network is a social structure made up of a set of actors (such as individuals or organizations) and the dyadic ties between these actors (such as relationships, connections, or interactions). A social network perspective is employed to model the structure of a social group, how this structure influences other variables, or how structures change over time. The study of these structures uses methods in social network analysis to identify influential nodes, local and global structures, and network dynamics. |
| Psychoanalytic literary criticism | Psychoanalytic literary criticism refers to literary criticism which, in method, concept, theory is influenced by the tradition of psychoanalysis begun by Sigmund Freud. Psychoanalytic reading has been practiced since the early development of psychoanalysis itself, and has developed into a rich and heterogeneous interpretive tradition. |
| | It is a literary approach where critics see the text as if it were a kind of dream. |
| Abstraction | Abstraction is a process by which higher concepts are derived from the usage and classification of literal ('real' or 'concrete') concepts, first principles, or other methods. |

# Chapter 6. Nonverbal Communication

CHAPTER HIGHLIGHTS & NOTES: KEY TERMS, PEOPLE, PLACES, CONCEPTS

'An abstraction' is the product of this process - a concept that acts as a super-categorical noun for all subordinate concepts, and connects any related concepts as a group, field, or category.

Abstractions may be formed by reducing the information content of a concept or an observable phenomenon, typically to retain only information which is relevant for a particular purpose.

**Emblem**

An emblem is a pictorial image, abstract or representational, that epitomizes a concept -- e.g., a moral truth, or an allegory -- or that represents a person, such as a king or saint.

Distinction: emblem and symbol

The words emblem and symbol often appear interchangeably in day-to-day conversation without causing undue confusion. A distinction between the two may seem unnecessarily fastidious.

**Kinesics**

Kinesics is the interpretation of body language such as facial expressions and gestures -- or, more formally, non-verbal behavior related to movement, either of any part of the body or the body as a whole. Birdwhistell's work

The term was first used (in 1952) by Ray Birdwhistell, an anthropologist who wished to study how people communicate through posture, gesture, stance, and movement. Part of Birdwhistell's work involved making film of people in social situations and analyzing them to show different levels of communication not clearly seen otherwise.

**ADHD**

Attention-deficit hyperactivity disorder (ADHD or AD/HD) is a neurobehavioral developmental disorder. ADHD is primarily characterized by 'the co-existence of attentional problems and hyperactivity, with each behavior occurring infrequently alone.' While symptoms may appear to be innocent and merely annoying nuisances to observers, 'if left untreated, the persistent and pervasive effects of ADHD symptoms can insidiously and severely interfere with one's ability to get the most out of education, fulfill one's potential in the workplace, establish and maintain interpersonal relationships, and maintain a generally positive sense of self.'[:p.2]

ADHD is the most commonly studied and diagnosed psychiatric disorder in children, affecting about 3 to 5% of children globally with symptoms starting before seven years of age. ADHD is a common chronic disorder in children with 30 to 50% of those individuals diagnosed in childhood continuing to have symptoms into adulthood.

**Internet**

The Internet is a global system of interconnected computer networks that use the standard Internet Protocol Suite (TCP/IP) to serve billions of users worldwide. It is a network of networks that consists of millions of private, public, academic, business, and government networks, of local to global scope, that are linked by a broad array of electronic, wireless and optical networking technologies.

# Chapter 6. Nonverbal Communication

CHAPTER HIGHLIGHTS & NOTES: KEY TERMS, PEOPLE, PLACES, CONCEPTS

| | |
|---|---|
| Prevention | Prevention refers to:<br><br>· Preventive medicine · Hazard Prevention, the process of risk study and elimination and mitigation in emergency management · Risk Prevention · Risk management · Preventive maintenance · Crime Prevention<br><br>· Prevention, an album by Scottish band De Rosa · Prevention a magazine about health in the United States · Prevent (company), a textile company from Slovenia · Prevent (campaign), an anti-radicalization program in the United Kingdom |
| Direct marketing | Direct marketing is a form of advertising that reaches its audience without using traditional formal channels of advertising, such as TV, newspapers or radio. Businesses communicate straight to the consumer with advertising techniques such as fliers, catalogue distribution, promotional letters, and street advertising.<br><br>Direct Advertising is a sub-discipline and type of marketing. |
| Enunciation | In phonetics, enunciation is the act of speaking. Good enunciation is the act of speaking clearly and concisely. The opposite of good enunciation is mumbling or slurring. |
| Filler | In linguistics, a filler is a sound or word that is spoken in conversation by one participant to signal to others that he/she has paused to think but is not yet finished speaking. These are not to be confused with placeholder names, such as thingamajig, which refer to objects or people whose names are temporarily forgotten, irrelevant, or unknown. Different languages have different characteristic filler sounds; in English, the most common filler sounds are uh /?/, er /?/ and um /?m/. |
| Inflection | In grammar, inflection is the modification of a word to express different grammatical categories such as tense, grammatical mood, grammatical voice, aspect, person, number, gender and case. Conjugation is the inflection of verbs; declension is the inflection of nouns, adjectives and pronouns.<br><br>An inflection expresses one or more grammatical categories with an explicitly stated prefix, suffix, or infix or other internal modification such as a vowel change. |
| Pronunciation | Pronunciation refers to the way a word or a language is spoken, or the manner in which someone utters a word. If one is said to have 'correct pronunciation', then it refers to both within a particular dialect. |

# Chapter 6. Nonverbal Communication

CHAPTER HIGHLIGHTS & NOTES: KEY TERMS, PEOPLE, PLACES, CONCEPTS

| | |
|---|---|
| Speech | Speech is the vocalized form of human communication. It is based upon the syntactic combination of lexicals and names that are drawn from very large (usually to about 10,000 different words) vocabularies. Each spoken word is created out of the phonetic combination of a limited set of vowel and consonant speech sound units. |
| Gender role | Gender roles refer to the set of social and behavioral norms that are considered to be socially appropriate for individuals of a specific sex in the context of a specific culture, which differ widely between cultures and over time. There are differences of opinion as to whether observed gender differences in behavior and personality characteristics are, at least in part, due to cultural or social factors, and therefore, the product of socialization experiences, or to what extent gender differences are due to biological and physiological differences.<br><br>Views on gender-based differentiation in the workplace and in interpersonal relationships have often undergone profound changes as a result of feminist and/or economic influences, but there are still considerable differences in gender roles in almost all societies. |
| Proxemics | The term proxemics was introduced by anthropologist Edward T. Hall in 1966. Proxemics is the study of set measurable distances between people as they interact. The effects of proxemics, according to Hall, can be summarized by the following loose rule:<br><br>In animals, German zoologist Heini Heidger had distinguished between flight distance (run boundary), critical distance (attack boundary), personal distance (distance separating members of non-contact species, as a pair of swans), and social distance (intraspecies communication distance). Hall reasoned that, with very few exceptions, flight distance and critical distance have been eliminated in human reactions, and thus interviewed hundreds of people to determine modified criteria for human interactions. |
| Sexual attraction | Sexual attraction is attraction on the basis of sexual desire or the quality of arousing such interest. Sexual attractiveness or sex appeal refers to an individual's ability to attract the sexual or erotic interest of another person, and is a factor in sexual selection or mate choice. The attraction can be to the physical or other qualities or traits of a person, or to such qualities in the context in which they appear. |
| Academies | From the seventeenth century to the early part of the twentieth century, artistic production in France was controlled by artistic academies which organized official exhibitions called salons.<br><br>In France, 'academies' are institutions and learned societies which monitor, foster, critique and protect French cultural production. academies first began to appear in France in the Renaissance, inspired by Italian models (such as the academy around Marsilio Ficino). |

## Chapter 6. Nonverbal Communication

**CHAPTER HIGHLIGHTS & NOTES: KEY TERMS, PEOPLE, PLACES, CONCEPTS**

| | |
|---|---|
| Halo effect | T halo effect is defined as 't influence of a global evaluation on evaluations of individual attributes of a person'. (Nisbett & Wilson, 1977). More simply it is t transfer of t beliefs about a good trait a person may have onto tir otr traits. |
| Chronemics | Chronemics is the study of the use of time in nonverbal communication. The way we perceive time, structure our time and react to time is a powerful communication tool, and helps set the stage for the communication process. Across cultures, time perception plays a large role in the nonverbal communication process. |
| Clubflyer | A Clubflyer or flyer (also spelled flier or called handbill) is a single page leaflet advertising a nightclub, event, service, community communication. |
| Autonomy | Autonomy is a concept found in moral, political, and bioethical philosophy. Within these contexts, it refers to the capacity of a rational individual to make an informed, un-coerced decision. In moral and political philosophy, autonomy is often used as the basis for determining moral responsibility for one's actions. |
| Interpreting | Language interpretation is the practice of facilitating oral and sign-language communication, either simultaneously or consecutively, between two or more users of different languages. Functionally, interpreting and interpretation are both descriptive words for this process.<br><br>In professional practice, interpreting denotes the act of facilitating communication from one language form into its equivalent, or approximate equivalent, in another language form. |

**CHAPTER QUIZ: KEY TERMS, PEOPLE, PLACES, CONCEPTS**

1. _____ is the activity of conveying information. _____ has been derived from the Latin word 'communis', meaning to share. _____ requires a sender, a message, and an intended recipient, although the receiver need not be present or aware of the sender's intent to communicate at the time of _____; thus _____ can occur across vast distances in time and space.

    a. Communication
    b. Communication endpoint
    c. Communication for Development
    d. Communication for social change

2. . Language interpretation is the practice of facilitating oral and sign-language communication, either simultaneously or consecutively, between two or more users of different languages.

## Chapter 6. Nonverbal Communication

CHAPTER QUIZ: KEY TERMS, PEOPLE, PLACES, CONCEPTS

Functionally, _____ and interpretation are both descriptive words for this process.

In professional practice, _____ denotes the act of facilitating communication from one language form into its equivalent, or approximate equivalent, in another language form.

a. Information design
b. Alphaphonetic pronunciation
c. Interpreting
d. Error analysis

3. _____ is usually understood as the process of communication through sending and receiving wordless (mostly visual) messages between people. Messages can be communicated through gestures and touch, by body language or posture, by facial expression and eye contact. Nonverbal messages could also be communicated through material exponential; meaning, objects or artifacts(such as clothing, hairstyles or architecture).

a. Paralanguage
b. Nonverbal communication
c. Reply
d. Sigh

4. _____ is a meeting of the eyes between two individuals.

In human beings, _____ is a form of nonverbal communication and is thought to have a large influence on social behavior. Coined in the early to mid-1960s, the term has come in the West to often define the act as a meaningful and important sign of confidence and social communication.

a. Open outcry
b. Eye contact
c. Communication for Development
d. Communication for social change

5. A _____ results from one or more motions or positions of the muscles of the face. These movements convey the emotional state of the individual to observers. _____s are a form of nonverbal communication.

a. Baka
b. Facial expression
c. Bar joke
d. Barbara Bauer Literary Agency

**ANSWER KEY**
Chapter 6. Nonverbal Communication

1. a
2. c
3. b
4. b
5. b

## You can take the complete Chapter Practice Test

**for Chapter 6. Nonverbal Communication**
on all key terms, persons, places, and concepts.

## Online 99 Cents

### http://www.epub21.1.20820.6.cram101.com/

Use www.Cram101.com for all your study needs

including Cram101's online interactive problem solving labs in

chemistry, statistics, mathematics, and more.

# Chapter 7. Listening

CHAPTER OUTLINE: KEY TERMS, PEOPLE, PLACES, CONCEPTS

- National Day of Listening
- FINANCIAL
- Communication
- Misconception
- Bermuda Triangle
- Autonomy
- Paraphrasing
- Informational listening
- ADHD
- Information overload
- Direct marketing
- Direct Marketing Association
- Confirmation bias
- Probabilities
- Statement

# Chapter 7. Listening

CHAPTER HIGHLIGHTS & NOTES: KEY TERMS, PEOPLE, PLACES, CONCEPTS

| | |
|---|---|
| National Day of Listening | The National Day of Listening is an unofficial day of observance where Americans are encouraged to set aside time to record the stories of their families, friends, and local communities. It was first launched by the national oral history project StoryCorps in 2008 and now recurs on the Friday after Thanksgiving Day, when families are more likely to spend time together. It was proposed as an alternative to 'Black Friday', a day many businesses see as a high volume pre-Christmas sale day. |
| FINANCIAL | FINANCIAL is the weekly English-language newspaper with offices in Tbilisi, Georgia and Kiev, Ukraine. Published by Intelligence Group LLC, FINANCIAL is focused on opinion leaders and top business decision-makers; It's about world's largest companies, investing, careers, and small business. It is distributed in Georgia and Ukraine. |
| Communication | Communication is the activity of conveying information. Communication has been derived from the Latin word 'communis', meaning to share. Communication requires a sender, a message, and an intended recipient, although the receiver need not be present or aware of the sender's intent to communicate at the time of communication; thus communication can occur across vast distances in time and space. |
| Misconception | A Misconception happens when a person believes in a concept which is objectively false.<br><br>Due to the subjective nature of humanity, it can be assumed that everyone has some kind of Misconception This postulates to 'no-one has perfect knowledge' and 'no-one has a perfect mental representation of the world.' If a concept cannot be proven to be either true or false, then it cannot be claimed that disbelievers have a Misconception of the concept by believers, no matter how much the believers want a concept to be true (and vice versa.) |
| Bermuda Triangle | The Bermuda Triangle is a region in the western part of the North Atlantic Ocean in which a number of aircraft and surface vessels are alleged to have mysteriously disappeared and cannot be explained as human error, piracy, equipment failure, a suspension of the laws of physics, or activity by extraterrestrial beings.<br><br>A substantial body of documentation reveals, however, that a significant portion of the allegedly mysterious incidents have been inaccurately reported or embellished by later authors, and numerous official agencies have stated that the number and nature of disappearances in the region is similar to any other area of ocean. |
| Autonomy | Autonomy is a concept found in moral, political, and bioethical philosophy. Within these contexts, it refers to the capacity of a rational individual to make an informed, un-coerced decision. In moral and political philosophy, autonomy is often used as the basis for determining moral responsibility for one's actions. |

# Chapter 7. Listening

**CHAPTER HIGHLIGHTS & NOTES: KEY TERMS, PEOPLE, PLACES, CONCEPTS**

| | |
|---|---|
| Paraphrasing | Paraphrase is restatement of a text or passages, using other words. The term 'paraphrase' derives via the Latin 'paraphrasis' from the Greek para phraseïn, meaning 'additional manner of expression'. The act of Paraphrasing is also called 'paraphrasis.' |
| | A paraphrase typically explains or clarifies the text that is being paraphrased. |
| Informational listening | The process of informational listening focuses on the abity of an individual to understand a speaker's message. It is a huge part of everyday life, and faing to understand the concept of informational listening can be very detrimental to one's contribution to society, and indeed, detrimental to quality of life in general. Much of the listening people engage in on a regular basis falls under the blanket of listening for information. |
| ADHD | Attention-deficit hyperactivity disorder (ADHD or AD/HD) is a neurobehavioral developmental disorder. ADHD is primarily characterized by 'the co-existence of attentional problems and hyperactivity, with each behavior occurring infrequently alone.' While symptoms may appear to be innocent and merely annoying nuisances to observers, 'if left untreated, the persistent and pervasive effects of ADHD symptoms can insidiously and severely interfere with one's ability to get the most out of education, fulfill one's potential in the workplace, establish and maintain interpersonal relationships, and maintain a generally positive sense of self.':p.2 |
| | ADHD is the most commonly studied and diagnosed psychiatric disorder in children, affecting about 3 to 5% of children globally with symptoms starting before seven years of age. ADHD is a common chronic disorder in children with 30 to 50% of those individuals diagnosed in childhood continuing to have symptoms into adulthood. |
| Information overload | 'Information overload' is a term popularized by Alvin Toffler in his bestselling 1970 book Future Shock. It refers to the difficulty a person can have understanding an issue and making decisions that can be caused by the presence of too much information. The term itself is mentioned in a 1964 book by Bertram Gross, The Managing of Organizations. |
| Direct marketing | Direct marketing is a form of advertising that reaches its audience without using traditional formal channels of advertising, such as TV, newspapers or radio. Businesses communicate straight to the consumer with advertising techniques such as fliers, catalogue distribution, promotional letters, and street advertising. |
| | Direct Advertising is a sub-discipline and type of marketing. |
| Direct Marketing Association | Direct Marketing Association (DMA) is a trade organization which seeks to advance all channels of direct marketing. DMA was founded in 1917. It is based in the United States, but its members include companies from 48 other countries as well, including half of the Fortune 100 companies, as well as nonprofit organizations. |

# Chapter 7. Listening

CHAPTER HIGHLIGHTS & NOTES: KEY TERMS, PEOPLE, PLACES, CONCEPTS

| | |
|---|---|
| Confirmation bias | Confirmation bias is a tendency of people to favor information that confirms their beliefs or hypotheses. People display this bias when they gather or remember information selectively, or when they interpret it in a biased way. The effect is stronger for emotionally charged issues and for deeply entrenched beliefs. |
| Probabilities | Probability is a way of expressing knowledge or belief that an event will occur or has occurred. In mathematics the concept has been given an exact meaning in probability theory, that is used extensively in such areas of study as mathematics, statistics, finance, gambling, science, and philosophy to draw conclusions about the likelihood of potential events and the underlying mechanics of complex systems. <br><br> The word probability does not have a consistent direct definition. In fact, there are sixteen broad categories of probability interpretations, whose adherents possess different (and sometimes conflicting) views about the fundamental nature of probability: <br><br> · Frequentists talk about probabilities only when dealing with experiments that are random and well-defined. |
| Statement | Statement may refer to:•A kind of expression in language (linguistics)•Statement declarative sentence that is either true or false•Statement the smallest standalone element of an imperative programming language•'Statement' (song), 2008 song by the Japanese band Boris•Statements (album), 1962 album by jazz vibraphonist Milt Jackson•Financial statements, formal records of the financial activities of a business, person, or other entity•Mathematical statement, a statement in logic and mathematics•Political statement, any act or nonverbal form of communication that is intended to influence a decision to be made for or by a group•Press statement, written or recorded communication directed at members of the news media•Statement of Special Educational Needs, outlining specific provision needed for a child in England•a paper size also known as organizer L or half letter. |

# Chapter 7. Listening

CHAPTER QUIZ: KEY TERMS, PEOPLE, PLACES, CONCEPTS

1. The _____ is an unofficial day of observance where Americans are encouraged to set aside time to record the stories of their families, friends, and local communities. It was first launched by the national oral history project StoryCorps in 2008 and now recurs on the Friday after Thanksgiving Day, when families are more likely to spend time together. It was proposed as an alternative to 'Black Friday', a day many businesses see as a high volume pre-Christmas sale day.

   a. Personal archiving
   b. Queens Memory Project
   c. Slave narrative
   d. National Day of Listening

2. Attention-deficit hyperactivity disorder (_____ or AD/HD) is a neurobehavioral developmental disorder. _____ is primarily characterized by 'the co-existence of attentional problems and hyperactivity, with each behavior occurring infrequently alone.' While symptoms may appear to be innocent and merely annoying nuisances to observers, 'if left untreated, the persistent and pervasive effects of _____ symptoms can insidiously and severely interfere with one's ability to get the most out of education, fulfill one's potential in the workplace, establish and maintain interpersonal relationships, and maintain a generally positive sense of self.':p.2

   _____ is the most commonly studied and diagnosed psychiatric disorder in children, affecting about 3 to 5% of children globally with symptoms starting before seven years of age. _____ is a common chronic disorder in children with 30 to 50% of those individuals diagnosed in childhood continuing to have symptoms into adulthood.

   a. attention deficit hyperactivity disorder
   b. ADHD
   c. Affine transformation
   d. Integrative communication theory

3. _____(DMA) is a trade organization which seeks to advance all channels of direct marketing. DMA was founded in 1917. It is based in the United States, but its members include companies from 48 other countries as well, including half of the Fortune 100 companies, as well as nonprofit organizations.

   The Direct Marketing Association provides a method for consumers to opt out of various kinds of direct marketing, including credit and insurance offers by mail, catalogs, magazines, and other direct mail offers.

   a. Direct Marketing Association
   b. Direct response television
   c. Dunhill International List Company
   d. DVD club

4. . _____ is the weekly English-language newspaper with offices in Tbilisi, Georgia and Kiev, Ukraine. Published by Intelligence Group LLC, _____ is focused on opinion leaders and top business decision-makers; It's about world's largest companies, investing, careers, and small business. It is distributed in Georgia and Ukraine.

   a. Baka

## Chapter 7. Listening

CHAPTER QUIZ: KEY TERMS, PEOPLE, PLACES, CONCEPTS

b. FINANCIAL

c. Slave narrative

d. Transgender Oral History Project

5. A _____ happens when a person believes in a concept which is objectively false.

Due to the subjective nature of humanity, it can be assumed that everyone has some kind of _____ This postulates to 'no-one has perfect knowledge' and 'no-one has a perfect mental representation of the world.' If a concept cannot be proven to be either true or false, then it cannot be claimed that disbelievers have a _____ of the concept by believers, no matter how much the believers want a concept to be true (and vice versa.)

a. Consequent

b. Baka

c. Misconception

d. Communication for social change

### ANSWER KEY
### Chapter 7. Listening

1. d
2. b
3. a
4. b
5. c

## You can take the complete Chapter Practice Test

### for Chapter 7. Listening

on all key terms, persons, places, and concepts.

## Online 99 Cents

### http://www.epub21.1.20820.7.cram101.com/

Use www.Cram101.com for all your study needs

including Cram101's online interactive problem solving labs in

chemistry, statistics, mathematics, and more.

# Chapter 8. Emotion
CHAPTER OUTLINE: KEY TERMS, PEOPLE, PLACES, CONCEPTS

- Direct marketing
- Facial expression
- Communication
- Gender role
- Social network
- Society
- FINANCIAL
- Emotional expression
- Emotional contagion
- Sexual attraction
- Personal network
- Spelling bee
- Agreeableness
- Emotional intelligence

# Chapter 8. Emotion

CHAPTER HIGHLIGHTS & NOTES: KEY TERMS, PEOPLE, PLACES, CONCEPTS

| | |
|---|---|
| Direct marketing | Direct marketing is a form of advertising that reaches its audience without using traditional formal channels of advertising, such as TV, newspapers or radio. Businesses communicate straight to the consumer with advertising techniques such as fliers, catalogue distribution, promotional letters, and street advertising.<br><br>Direct Advertising is a sub-discipline and type of marketing. |
| Facial expression | A Facial expression results from one or more motions or positions of the muscles of the face. These movements convey the emotional state of the individual to observers. Facial expressions are a form of nonverbal communication. |
| Communication | Communication is the activity of conveying information. Communication has been derived from the Latin word 'communis', meaning to share. Communication requires a sender, a message, and an intended recipient, although the receiver need not be present or aware of the sender's intent to communicate at the time of communication; thus communication can occur across vast distances in time and space. |
| Gender role | Gender roles refer to the set of social and behavioral norms that are considered to be socially appropriate for individuals of a specific sex in the context of a specific culture, which differ widely between cultures and over time. There are differences of opinion as to whether observed gender differences in behavior and personality characteristics are, at least in part, due to cultural or social factors, and therefore, the product of socialization experiences, or to what extent gender differences are due to biological and physiological differences.<br><br>Views on gender-based differentiation in the workplace and in interpersonal relationships have often undergone profound changes as a result of feminist and/or economic influences, but there are still considerable differences in gender roles in almost all societies. |
| Social network | A social network is a social structure made up of a set of actors (such as individuals or organizations) and the dyadic ties between these actors (such as relationships, connections, or interactions). A social network perspective is employed to model the structure of a social group, how this structure influences other variables, or how structures change over time. The study of these structures uses methods in social network analysis to identify influential nodes, local and global structures, and network dynamics. |
| Society | A society, is a group of people related to each other through persistent relations, or a large social grouping sharing the same geographical or virtual territory, subject to the same political authority and dominant cultural expectations. Human societies are characterized by patterns of relationships (social relations) between individuals who share a distinctive culture and institutions; a given society may be described as the sum total of such relationships among its constituent members. |

# Chapter 8. Emotion

CHAPTER HIGHLIGHTS & NOTES: KEY TERMS, PEOPLE, PLACES, CONCEPTS

| | |
|---|---|
| FINANCIAL | FINANCIAL is the weekly English-language newspaper with offices in Tbilisi, Georgia and Kiev, Ukraine. Published by Intelligence Group LLC, FINANCIAL is focused on opinion leaders and top business decision-makers; It's about world's largest companies, investing, careers, and small business. It is distributed in Georgia and Ukraine. |
| Emotional expression | In psychology, Emotional expression is observable verbal and nonverbal behaviour that communicates emotion. Emotional expression can occur with or without self-awareness. An individual can control such expression, to some extent, and may have deliberate intent in displaying it. |
| Emotional contagion | Emotional contagion is the tendency to catch and feel emotions that are similar to and associated with those of others. One view developed by John Cacioppo of the underlying mhanism is that it represents a tendency to mimic and synchronize facial expressions, vocalizations, postures, and movements with those of another person automatically and, consequently, to converge emotionally. A broader definition of the phenomenon was suggested by Sigal G. Barsade--'a process in which a person or group influences the emotions or behavior of another person or group through the conscious or unconscious induction of emotion states and behavioral attitudes'. |
| Sexual attraction | Sexual attraction is attraction on the basis of sexual desire or the quality of arousing such interest. Sexual attractiveness or sex appeal refers to an individual's ability to attract the sexual or erotic interest of another person, and is a factor in sexual selection or mate choice. The attraction can be to the physical or other qualities or traits of a person, or to such qualities in the context in which they appear. |
| Personal network | A personal network is a set of human contacts known to an individual, with whom that individual would expect to interact at intervals to support a given set of activities.<br><br>Personal networks are intended to be mutually beneficial--extending the concept of teamwork beyond the immediate peer group. The term is usually encountered in the workplace, though it could apply equally to other pursuits outside work. |
| Spelling bee | A spelling bee is a competition where contestants, usually children, are asked to spell English words. The concept is thought to have originated in the United States. Today, National Spelling Bee competitions for English are held in the United States, United Kingdom, Australia, New Zealand, Canada, Indonesia and India among others. |
| Agreeableness | Agreeableness is a tendency to be pleasant and accommodating in social situations. In contemporary personality psychology, agreeableness is one of the five major dimensions of personality structure, reflecting individual differences in concern for cooperation and social harmony. |

# Chapter 8. Emotion

## CHAPTER HIGHLIGHTS & NOTES: KEY TERMS, PEOPLE, PLACES, CONCEPTS

| | |
|---|---|
| Emotional intelligence | Emotional intelligence describes the ability, capacity, skill or, in the case of the trait Emotional intelligence model, a self-perceived grand ability to identify, assess, manage and control the emotions of one's self, of others, and of groups. Different models have been proposed for the definition of Emotional intelligence and disagreement exists as to how the term should be used. Despite these disagreements, which are often highly technical, the ability Emotional intelligence and trait Emotional intelligence models (but not the mixed models) enjoy support in the literature and have successful applications in different domains. |

## CHAPTER QUIZ: KEY TERMS, PEOPLE, PLACES, CONCEPTS

1. A _____, is a group of people related to each other through persistent relations, or a large social grouping sharing the same geographical or virtual territory, subject to the same political authority and dominant cultural expectations. Human societies are characterized by patterns of relationships (social relations) between individuals who share a distinctive culture and institutions; a given _____ may be described as the sum total of such relationships among its constituent members. In the social sciences, a larger _____ often evinces stratification and/or dominance patterns in subgroups.

    a. Society
    b. Sociotope
    c. Sodality
    d. Somatology

2. _____ is the weekly English-language newspaper with offices in Tbilisi, Georgia and Kiev, Ukraine. Published by Intelligence Group LLC, _____ is focused on opinion leaders and top business decision-makers; It's about world's largest companies, investing, careers, and small business. It is distributed in Georgia and Ukraine.

    a. Baka
    b. Calvin Veltman
    c. FINANCIAL
    d. Vernacular orientation

3. _____ describes the ability, capacity, skill or, in the case of the trait _____ model, a self-perceived grand ability to identify, assess, manage and control the emotions of one's self, of others, and of groups. Different models have been proposed for the definition of _____ and disagreement exists as to how the term should be used. Despite these disagreements, which are often highly technical, the ability _____ and trait _____ models (but not the mixed models) enjoy support in the literature and have successful applications in different domains.

    a. ad Herennium
    b. Emotional intelligence

# Chapter 8. Emotion

**CHAPTER QUIZ: KEY TERMS, PEOPLE, PLACES, CONCEPTS**

    c. Airport code
    d. Spelling Bee of Canada

4. _____ is a form of advertising that reaches its audience without using traditional formal channels of advertising, such as TV, newspapers or radio. Businesses communicate straight to the consumer with advertising techniques such as fliers, catalogue distribution, promotional letters, and street advertising.

   Direct Advertising is a sub-discipline and type of marketing.

    a. Direct marketing
    b. Relationship marketing
    c. Baka
    d. Band-pass filter

5. In psychology, _____ is observable verbal and nonverbal behaviour that communicates emotion. _____ can occur with or without self-awareness. An individual can control such expression, to some extent, and may have deliberate intent in displaying it.

    a. ad Herennium
    b. Calvin Veltman
    c. Vernacular
    d. Emotional expression

**ANSWER KEY**
**Chapter 8. Emotion**

1. a
2. c
3. b
4. a
5. d

**You can take the complete Chapter Practice Test**

**for Chapter 8. Emotion**
on all key terms, persons, places, and concepts.

**Online 99 Cents**

**http://www.epub21.1.20820.8.cram101.com/**

Use www.Cram101.com for all your study needs

including Cram101's online interactive problem solving labs in

chemistry, statistics, mathematics, and more.

# Chapter 9. Interpersonal Communication in Friendships and Professional R

CHAPTER OUTLINE: KEY TERMS, PEOPLE, PLACES, CONCEPTS

- Aristotle
- Interpersonal communication
- Personal network
- Spelling bee
- Communication
- Symmetry
- Internet
- Predicted outcome value theory
- Uncertainty reduction theory
- Autonomy
- Comparison
- Social exchange theory
- Othello error
- Equity theory
- Gender role
- Sexual attraction

Cram101.com for Practice Tests

# Chapter 9. Interpersonal Communication in Friendships and Professional Relationships

CHAPTER HIGHLIGHTS & NOTES: KEY TERMS, PEOPLE, PLACES, CONCEPTS

| | |
|---|---|
| Aristotle | Aristotle was a Greek philosopher, a student of Plato and teacher of Alexander the Great. His writings cover many subjects, including physics, metaphysics, poetry, theater, music, logic, rhetoric, linguistics, politics, government, ethics, biology, and zoology. Together with Plato and Socrates (Plato's teacher), Aristotle is one of the most important founding figures in Western philosophy. |
| Interpersonal communication | Interpersonal communication is usually defined by communication scholars in numerous ways, usually describing participants who are dependent upon one another. It can involve one on one conversations or individuals interacting with many people within a society. It helps us understand how and why people behave and communicate in different ways to construct and negotiate a social reality. |
| Personal network | A personal network is a set of human contacts known to an individual, with whom that individual would expect to interact at intervals to support a given set of activities.<br><br>Personal networks are intended to be mutually beneficial--extending the concept of teamwork beyond the immediate peer group. The term is usually encountered in the workplace, though it could apply equally to other pursuits outside work. |
| Spelling bee | A spelling bee is a competition where contestants, usually children, are asked to spell English words. The concept is thought to have originated in the United States. Today, National Spelling Bee competitions for English are held in the United States, United Kingdom, Australia, New Zealand, Canada, Indonesia and India among others. |
| Communication | Communication is the activity of conveying information. Communication has been derived from the Latin word 'communis', meaning to share. Communication requires a sender, a message, and an intended recipient, although the receiver need not be present or aware of the sender's intent to communicate at the time of communication; thus communication can occur across vast distances in time and space. |
| Symmetry | Symmetry generally conveys two primary meanings. The first is an imprecise sense of harmonious or aesthetically pleasing proportionality and balance; such that it reflects beauty or perfection. The second meaning is a precise and well-defined concept of balance or 'patterned self-similarity' that can be demonstrated or proved according to the rules of a formal system: by geometry, through physics or otherwise. |
| Internet | The Internet is a global system of interconnected computer networks that use the standard Internet Protocol Suite (TCP/IP) to serve billions of users worldwide. It is a network of networks that consists of millions of private, public, academic, business, and government networks, of local to global scope, that are linked by a broad array of electronic, wireless and optical networking technologies. |

# Chapter 9. Interpersonal Communication in Friendships and Professional Relationships

CHAPTER HIGHLIGHTS & NOTES: KEY TERMS, PEOPLE, PLACES, CONCEPTS

| | |
|---|---|
| Predicted outcome value theory | Predicted outcome value theory introduced in 1986 by Michael Sunnafrank, posits that people seek information in initial interactions and relationships to determine the benefits of interpersonal relationships by predicting the value of future outcomes whether negative or positive. If a person predicts a positive outcome in the relationship this can lead to increased attraction, however if a person predicts a negative outcome then he or she would pursue limited interaction or possibly relationship termination. The processes of predicted outcome value directly link to continued relationship development and communication as well as stronger attraction and intimacy within the relationship. |
| Uncertainty reduction theory | Uncertainty reduction theory originated from Charles Berger and Richard Calabrese in 1975. The goal for this theory was to predict and explain how communication is used to reduce the uncertainty among people involved in conversations with one another the first time they meet. This theory first aims to minimize the uncertainties that humans have about the world and the people within it. The theory then states that individuals will experience uncertainty on a regular basis and that the experience of uncertainty is an unpleasant one. |
| Autonomy | Autonomy is a concept found in moral, political, and bioethical philosophy. Within these contexts, it refers to the capacity of a rational individual to make an informed, un-coerced decision. In moral and political philosophy, autonomy is often used as the basis for determining moral responsibility for one's actions. |
| Comparison | Comparison, in grammar, is a property of adjectives and adverbs in most languages; it describes systems that distinguish the degree to which the modifier modifies its complement.<br><br>English, due to the complex etymology of its lexicon, has two parallel systems of comparison. One involves the suffixes -er (the 'comparative') and -est (the 'superlative'). |
| Social exchange theory | Social exchange theory is a social psychological and sociological perspective that explains social change and stability as a process of negotiated exchanges between parties. Social exchange theory posits that all human relationships are formed by the use of a subjective cost-benefit analysis and the comparison of alternatives. The theory has roots in economics, psychology and sociology. |
| Othello error | Othello error occurs when a suspicious observer discounts cues of truthfulness, given the observer's need to conform his/her observations of suspicions of deception. Essentially Othello error occurs 'when the lie catcher fails to consider that a truthful person who is under stress may appear to be lying.' (Ekman, 1985).<br><br>The term relates to the Shakespeare play in which Othello misinterprets Desdemona's reaction to Cassio's death. |

# Chapter 9. Interpersonal Communication in Friendships and Professional Relationships

CHAPTER HIGHLIGHTS & NOTES: KEY TERMS, PEOPLE, PLACES, CONCEPTS

| | |
|---|---|
| Equity theory | Equity theory is a theory that attempts to explain relational satisfaction in terms of perceptions of fair/unfair distributions of resources within interpersonal relationships. Considered one of the justice theories, equity theory was first developed in 1963 by John Stacey Adams, a workplace and behavioral psychologist, who asserted that employees seek to maintain equity bween the inputs that they bring to a job and the outcomes that they receive from it against the perceived inputs and outcomes of others (Adams, 1965). The belief is that people value fair treatment which causes them to be motivated to keep the fairness maintained within the relationships of their co-workers and the organization. |
| Gender role | Gender roles refer to the set of social and behavioral norms that are considered to be socially appropriate for individuals of a specific sex in the context of a specific culture, which differ widely between cultures and over time. There are differences of opinion as to whether observed gender differences in behavior and personality characteristics are, at least in part, due to cultural or social factors, and therefore, the product of socialization experiences, or to what extent gender differences are due to biological and physiological differences.<br><br>Views on gender-based differentiation in the workplace and in interpersonal relationships have often undergone profound changes as a result of feminist and/or economic influences, but there are still considerable differences in gender roles in almost all societies. |
| Sexual attraction | Sexual attraction is attraction on the basis of sexual desire or the quality of arousing such interest. Sexual attractiveness or sex appeal refers to an individual's ability to attract the sexual or erotic interest of another person, and is a factor in sexual selection or mate choice. The attraction can be to the physical or other qualities or traits of a person, or to such qualities in the context in which they appear. |

CHAPTER QUIZ: KEY TERMS, PEOPLE, PLACES, CONCEPTS

1. . _____s refer to the set of social and behavioral norms that are considered to be socially appropriate for individuals of a specific sex in the context of a specific culture, which differ widely between cultures and over time. There are differences of opinion as to whether observed gender differences in behavior and personality characteristics are, at least in part, due to cultural or social factors, and therefore, the product of socialization experiences, or to what extent gender differences are due to biological and physiological differences.

Views on gender-based differentiation in the workplace and in interpersonal relationships have often undergone profound changes as a result of feminist and/or economic influences, but there are still considerable differences in _____s in almost all societies.

a. Gender role
b. Group affective tone

# Chapter 9. Interpersonal Communication in Friendships and Professional Relationships

CHAPTER QUIZ: KEY TERMS, PEOPLE, PLACES, CONCEPTS

    c. Guanxi
    d. Guilt

2. _____ is a social psychological and sociological perspective that explains social change and stability as a process of negotiated exchanges between parties. _____ posits that all human relationships are formed by the use of a subjective cost-benefit analysis and the comparison of alternatives. The theory has roots in economics, psychology and sociology.

    a. Social penetration theory
    b. Uncertainty reduction theory
    c. Exploring
    d. Social exchange theory

3. _____ was a Greek philosopher, a student of Plato and teacher of Alexander the Great. His writings cover many subjects, including physics, metaphysics, poetry, theater, music, logic, rhetoric, linguistics, politics, government, ethics, biology, and zoology. Together with Plato and Socrates (Plato's teacher), _____ is one of the most important founding figures in Western philosophy.

    a. James A. Berlin
    b. Aristotle
    c. Gregory G. Colomb
    d. Robert T. Craig

4. _____ is usually defined by communication scholars in numerous ways, usually describing participants who are dependent upon one another. It can involve one on one conversations or individuals interacting with many people within a society. It helps us understand how and why people behave and communicate in different ways to construct and negotiate a social reality.

    a. Interpersonal communication
    b. Unconscious communication
    c. A-not-A question
    d. Ambiguity tolerance

5. A _____ is a set of human contacts known to an individual, with whom that individual would expect to interact at intervals to support a given set of activities.

_____s are intended to be mutually beneficial--extending the concept of teamwork beyond the immediate peer group. The term is usually encountered in the workplace, though it could apply equally to other pursuits outside work.

    a. Personal network
    b. RadCon
    c. Rhizome
    d. Science fiction fandom

**ANSWER KEY**
Chapter 9. Interpersonal Communication in Friendships and Professional Relationships

1. a
2. d
3. b
4. a
5. a

## You can take the complete Chapter Practice Test

for Chapter 9. Interpersonal Communication in Friendships and Professional Relationships
on all key terms, persons, places, and concepts.

### Online 99 Cents

http://www.epub21.1.20820.9.cram101.com/

Use www.Cram101.com for all your study needs

including Cram101's online interactive problem solving labs in

chemistry, statistics, mathematics, and more.

# Chapter 10. Interpersonal Communication in Romantic and Family Relations

CHAPTER OUTLINE: KEY TERMS, PEOPLE, PLACES, CONCEPTS

- Clubflyer
- FINANCIAL
- Intrapersonal communication
- Cyberstalking
- Autonomy
- Direct marketing
- Gender role
- Sexual attraction
- Interpersonal communication
- Internet
- Online
- Prevention
- Communication
- Nonverbal
- Nonverbal communication
- Verbal abuse

# Chapter 10. Interpersonal Communication in Romantic and Family Relationships

CHAPTER HIGHLIGHTS & NOTES: KEY TERMS, PEOPLE, PLACES, CONCEPTS

| | |
|---|---|
| Clubflyer | A Clubflyer or flyer (also spelled flier or called handbill) is a single page leaflet advertising a nightclub, event, service, community communication. |
| FINANCIAL | FINANCIAL is the weekly English-language newspaper with offices in Tbilisi, Georgia and Kiev, Ukraine. Published by Intelligence Group LLC, FINANCIAL is focused on opinion leaders and top business decision-makers; It's about world's largest companies, investing, careers, and small business. It is distributed in Georgia and Ukraine. |
| Intrapersonal communication | Intrapersonal communication is language use or thought internal to the communicator. It can be useful to envision intrapersonal communication occurring in the mind of the individual in a model which contains a sender, receiver, and feedback loop. <br><br> Although successful communication is generally defined as being between two or more individuals, issues concerning the useful nature of communicating with oneself and problems concerning communication with non-sentient entities such as computers have made some argue that this definition is too narrow. |
| Cyberstalking | Cyberstalking is the use of the Internet or other electronic means to stalk or harass an individual, a group of individuals, or an organization. It may include false accusations, monitoring, making threats, identity theft, damage to data or equipment, the solicitation of minors for sex, or gathering information in order to harass. The definition of 'harassment' must meet the criterion that a reasonable person, in possession of the same information, would regard it as sufficient to cause another reasonable person distress. |
| Autonomy | Autonomy is a concept found in moral, political, and bioethical philosophy. Within these contexts, it refers to the capacity of a rational individual to make an informed, un-coerced decision. In moral and political philosophy, autonomy is often used as the basis for determining moral responsibility for one's actions. |
| Direct marketing | Direct marketing is a form of advertising that reaches its audience without using traditional formal channels of advertising, such as TV, newspapers or radio. Businesses communicate straight to the consumer with advertising techniques such as fliers, catalogue distribution, promotional letters, and street advertising. <br><br> Direct Advertising is a sub-discipline and type of marketing. |
| Gender role | Gender roles refer to the set of social and behavioral norms that are considered to be socially appropriate for individuals of a specific sex in the context of a specific culture, which differ widely between cultures and over time. |

# Chapter 10. Interpersonal Communication in Romantic and Family Relationships

CHAPTER HIGHLIGHTS & NOTES: KEY TERMS, PEOPLE, PLACES, CONCEPTS

| | |
|---|---|
| | There are differences of opinion as to whether observed gender differences in behavior and personality characteristics are, at least in part, due to cultural or social factors, and therefore, the product of socialization experiences, or to what extent gender differences are due to biological and physiological differences.

Views on gender-based differentiation in the workplace and in interpersonal relationships have often undergone profound changes as a result of feminist and/or economic influences, but there are still considerable differences in gender roles in almost all societies. |
| Sexual attraction | Sexual attraction is attraction on the basis of sexual desire or the quality of arousing such interest. Sexual attractiveness or sex appeal refers to an individual's ability to attract the sexual or erotic interest of another person, and is a factor in sexual selection or mate choice. The attraction can be to the physical or other qualities or traits of a person, or to such qualities in the context in which they appear. |
| Interpersonal communication | Interpersonal communication is usually defined by communication scholars in numerous ways, usually describing participants who are dependent upon one another. It can involve one on one conversations or individuals interacting with many people within a society. It helps us understand how and why people behave and communicate in different ways to construct and negotiate a social reality. |
| Internet | The Internet is a global system of interconnected computer networks that use the standard Internet Protocol Suite (TCP/IP) to serve billions of users worldwide. It is a network of networks that consists of millions of private, public, academic, business, and government networks, of local to global scope, that are linked by a broad array of electronic, wireless and optical networking technologies. The Internet carries a vast range of information resources and services, such as the inter-linked hypertext documents of the World Wide Web (WWW) and the infrastructure to support electronic mail. |
| Online | The terms online and offline (also on-line and off-line) have specific meanings with respect to computer technology and telecommunication. In general, 'online' indicates a state of connectivity, while 'offline' indicates a disconnected state. In common usage, 'online' often refers to the Internet or the World Wide Web. |
| Prevention | Prevention refers to:

· Preventive medicine · Hazard Prevention, the process of risk study and elimination and mitigation in emergency management · Risk Prevention · Risk management · Preventive maintenance · Crime Prevention

· Prevention, an album by Scottish band De Rosa |

# Chapter 10. Interpersonal Communication in Romantic and Family Relationships

CHAPTER HIGHLIGHTS & NOTES: KEY TERMS, PEOPLE, PLACES, CONCEPTS

|  |  |
|---|---|
|  | · Prevention a magazine about health in the United States · Prevent (company), a textile company from Slovenia · Prevent (campaign), an anti-radicalization program in the United Kingdom |
| Communication | Communication is the activity of conveying information. Communication has been derived from the Latin word 'communis', meaning to share. Communication requires a sender, a message, and an intended recipient, although the receiver need not be present or aware of the sender's intent to communicate at the time of communication; thus communication can occur across vast distances in time and space. |
| Nonverbal | Nonverbal communications (NVC) is usually understood as the process of communication through sending and receiving wordless messages. i.e, language is not one source of communication, there are other means also. NVC can be communicated through gestures and touch (Haptic communication), by body language or posture, by facial expression and eye contact. |
| Nonverbal communication | Nonverbal communication is usually understood as the process of communication through sending and receiving wordless (mostly visual) messages between people. Messages can be communicated through gestures and touch, by body language or posture, by facial expression and eye contact. Nonverbal messages could also be communicated through material exponential; meaning, objects or artifacts(such as clothing, hairstyles or architecture). |
| Verbal abuse | Verbal abuse is a form of abusive behavior involving the use of language. It is a form of profanity that can occur with or without the use of expletives. While oral communication is the most common form of Verbal abuse, it includes abusive words in written form. |

CHAPTER QUIZ: KEY TERMS, PEOPLE, PLACES, CONCEPTS

1. _____ communications (NVC) is usually understood as the process of communication through sending and receiving wordless messages. i.e, language is not one source of communication, there are other means also. NVC can be communicated through gestures and touch (Haptic communication), by body language or posture, by facial expression and eye contact.

    a. Body language
    b. Body-to-body communication
    c. Nonverbal
    d. Dress code

2. . _____ is a form of advertising that reaches its audience without using traditional formal channels of advertising, such as TV, newspapers or radio. Businesses communicate straight to the consumer with advertising techniques such as fliers, catalogue distribution, promotional letters, and street advertising.

# Chapter 10. Interpersonal Communication in Romantic and Family Relationships

CHAPTER QUIZ: KEY TERMS, PEOPLE, PLACES, CONCEPTS

Direct Advertising is a sub-discipline and type of marketing.

a. Database marketing
b. Relationship marketing
c. Baka
d. Direct marketing

3. _____ is language use or thought internal to the communicator. It can be useful to envision _____ occurring in the mind of the individual in a model which contains a sender, receiver, and feedback loop.

Although successful communication is generally defined as being between two or more individuals, issues concerning the useful nature of communicating with oneself and problems concerning communication with non-sentient entities such as computers have made some argue that this definition is too narrow.

a. Intrapersonal communication
b. U and non-U English
c. I-message
d. Interactivity

4. _____ is the activity of conveying information. _____ has been derived from the Latin word 'communis', meaning to share. _____ requires a sender, a message, and an intended recipient, although the receiver need not be present or aware of the sender's intent to communicate at the time of _____; thus _____ can occur across vast distances in time and space.

a. Communication
b. Communication endpoint
c. Communication for Development
d. Communication for social change

5. A _____ or flyer (also spelled flier or called handbill) is a single page leaflet advertising a nightclub, event, service, community communication.

a. Clubflyer
b. Toleration
c. student
d. connotation

**ANSWER KEY**
Chapter 10. Interpersonal Communication in Romantic and Family Relationships

1. c
2. d
3. a
4. a
5. a

## You can take the complete Chapter Practice Test

for Chapter 10. Interpersonal Communication in Romantic and Family Relationships
on all key terms, persons, places, and concepts.

### Online 99 Cents

### http://www.epub21.1.20820.10.cram101.com/

Use www.Cram101.com for all your study needs

including Cram101's online interactive problem solving labs in

chemistry, statistics, mathematics, and more.

# Chapter 11. Interpersonal Conflict

CHAPTER OUTLINE: KEY TERMS, PEOPLE, PLACES, CONCEPTS

- Conflict management
- Procedural
- Restrictive
- Communication
- Intrapersonal communication
- Direct marketing
- Gender role
- Sexual attraction
- Online
- Psychoanalytic literary criticism
- Clubflyer
- Social network
- Autonomy

# Chapter 11. Interpersonal Conflict

CHAPTER HIGHLIGHTS & NOTES: KEY TERMS, PEOPLE, PLACES, CONCEPTS

| | |
|---|---|
| Conflict management | Conflict management involves implementing strategies to limit the negative aspects of conflict and to increase the positive aspects of conflict at a level equal to or higher than where the conflict is taking place. Furthermore, the aim of conflict management is to enhance learning and group outcomes (effectiveness or performance in organizational setting). It is not concerned with eliminating all conflict or avoiding conflict. |
| Procedural | A Procedural is a cross-genre type of literature, film, or television program involving a sequence of technical detail. A documentary film may be written in a procedural style to heighten narrative interest.

Types

Television

Fiction

In television, 'procedural' specifically refers to a genre of programs in which a problem is introduced, investigated and solved all within the same episode. |
| Restrictive | In semantics, a modifier is said to be restrictive (or defining) if it restricts the reference of its head. For example, in 'the red car is fancier than the blue one', red and blue are restrictive, because they restrict which cars car and one are referring to. ('The car is fancier than the one' would make little sense). |
| Communication | Communication is the activity of conveying information. Communication has been derived from the Latin word 'communis', meaning to share. Communication requires a sender, a message, and an intended recipient, although the receiver need not be present or aware of the sender's intent to communicate at the time of communication; thus communication can occur across vast distances in time and space. |
| Intrapersonal communication | Intrapersonal communication is language use or thought internal to the communicator. It can be useful to envision intrapersonal communication occurring in the mind of the individual in a model which contains a sender, receiver, and feedback loop.

Although successful communication is generally defined as being between two or more individuals, issues concerning the useful nature of communicating with oneself and problems concerning communication with non-sentient entities such as computers have made some argue that this definition is too narrow. |
| Direct marketing | Direct marketing is a form of advertising that reaches its audience without using traditional formal channels of advertising, such as TV, newspapers or radio. |

# Chapter 11. Interpersonal Conflict

CHAPTER HIGHLIGHTS & NOTES: KEY TERMS, PEOPLE, PLACES, CONCEPTS

| | |
|---|---|
| | Businesses communicate straight to the consumer with advertising techniques such as fliers, catalogue distribution, promotional letters, and street advertising. |
| | Direct Advertising is a sub-discipline and type of marketing. |
| Gender role | Gender roles refer to the set of social and behavioral norms that are considered to be socially appropriate for individuals of a specific sex in the context of a specific culture, which differ widely between cultures and over time. There are differences of opinion as to whether observed gender differences in behavior and personality characteristics are, at least in part, due to cultural or social factors, and therefore, the product of socialization experiences, or to what extent gender differences are due to biological and physiological differences. |
| | Views on gender-based differentiation in the workplace and in interpersonal relationships have often undergone profound changes as a result of feminist and/or economic influences, but there are still considerable differences in gender roles in almost all societies. |
| Sexual attraction | Sexual attraction is attraction on the basis of sexual desire or the quality of arousing such interest. Sexual attractiveness or sex appeal refers to an individual's ability to attract the sexual or erotic interest of another person, and is a factor in sexual selection or mate choice. The attraction can be to the physical or other qualities or traits of a person, or to such qualities in the context in which they appear. |
| Online | The terms online and offline (also on-line and off-line) have specific meanings with respect to computer technology and telecommunication. In general, 'online' indicates a state of connectivity, while 'offline' indicates a disconnected state. In common usage, 'online' often refers to the Internet or the World Wide Web. |
| Psychoanalytic literary criticism | Psychoanalytic literary criticism refers to literary criticism which, in method, concept, theory is influenced by the tradition of psychoanalysis begun by Sigmund Freud. Psychoanalytic reading has been practiced since the early development of psychoanalysis itself, and has developed into a rich and heterogeneous interpretive tradition. |
| | It is a literary approach where critics see the text as if it were a kind of dream. |
| Clubflyer | A Clubflyer or flyer (also spelled flier or called handbill) is a single page leaflet advertising a nightclub, event, service, community communication. |
| Social network | A social network is a social structure made up of a set of actors (such as individuals or organizations) and the dyadic ties between these actors (such as relationships, connections, or interactions). A social network perspective is employed to model the structure of a social group, how this structure influences other variables, or how structures change over time. |

# Chapter 11. Interpersonal Conflict

## CHAPTER HIGHLIGHTS & NOTES: KEY TERMS, PEOPLE, PLACES, CONCEPTS

| | |
|---|---|
| Autonomy | Autonomy is a concept found in moral, political, and bioethical philosophy. Within these contexts, it refers to the capacity of a rational individual to make an informed, un-coerced decision. In moral and political philosophy, autonomy is often used as the basis for determining moral responsibility for one's actions. |

## CHAPTER QUIZ: KEY TERMS, PEOPLE, PLACES, CONCEPTS

1. _____ involves implementing strategies to limit the negative aspects of conflict and to increase the positive aspects of conflict at a level equal to or higher than where the conflict is taking place. Furthermore, the aim of _____ is to enhance learning and group outcomes (effectiveness or performance in organizational setting). It is not concerned with eliminating all conflict or avoiding conflict.

    a. Conflict management
    b. Band-pass filter
    c. Bar joke
    d. Barbara Bauer Literary Agency

2. A _____ is a social structure made up of a set of actors (such as individuals or organizations) and the dyadic ties between these actors (such as relationships, connections, or interactions). A _____ perspective is employed to model the structure of a social group, how this structure influences other variables, or how structures change over time. The study of these structures uses methods in _____ analysis to identify influential nodes, local and global structures, and network dynamics.

    a. Social network
    b. Social television
    c. SpoCon
    d. Steamcon

3. A _____ or flyer (also spelled flier or called handbill) is a single page leaflet advertising a nightclub, event, service, community communication.

    a. manuscript
    b. Clubflyer
    c. student
    d. connotation

4. . _____s refer to the set of social and behavioral norms that are considered to be socially appropriate for individuals of a specific sex in the context of a specific culture, which differ widely between cultures and over time.

## Chapter 11. Interpersonal Conflict

CHAPTER QUIZ: KEY TERMS, PEOPLE, PLACES, CONCEPTS

There are differences of opinion as to whether observed gender differences in behavior and personality characteristics are, at least in part, due to cultural or social factors, and therefore, the product of socialization experiences, or to what extent gender differences are due to biological and physiological differences.

Views on gender-based differentiation in the workplace and in interpersonal relationships have often undergone profound changes as a result of feminist and/or economic influences, but there are still considerable differences in _____s in almost all societies.

a. Greater Good Science Center
b. Group affective tone
c. Gender role
d. Guilt

5. A _____ is a cross-genre type of literature, film, or television program involving a sequence of technical detail. A documentary film may be written in a _____ style to heighten narrative interest.

Types

Television

Fiction

In television, '_____' specifically refers to a genre of programs in which a problem is introduced, investigated and solved all within the same episode.

a. Procedural
b. Prosimetrum
c. Psychological novel
d. Psychological thriller

**ANSWER KEY**
**Chapter 11. Interpersonal Conflict**

1. a
2. a
3. b
4. c
5. a

## You can take the complete Chapter Practice Test

### for Chapter 11. Interpersonal Conflict
on all key terms, persons, places, and concepts.

### Online 99 Cents

### http://www.epub21.1.20820.11.cram101.com/

Use www.Cram101.com for all your study needs

including Cram101's online interactive problem solving labs in

chemistry, statistics, mathematics, and more.

# Chapter 12. Deceptive Communication

CHAPTER OUTLINE: KEY TERMS, PEOPLE, PLACES, CONCEPTS

- Broadband
- FINANCIAL
- Othello error
- Procedural
- Exposition Boy
- Clubflyer
- Restrictive
- Perjury
- E-mail
- Online
- Diversity
- Communication
- Dissimulation
- Equivocation
- Filler
- Psychoanalytic literary criticism
- Speech error
- Interpersonal deception theory

# Chapter 12. Deceptive Communication

CHAPTER HIGHLIGHTS & NOTES: KEY TERMS, PEOPLE, PLACES, CONCEPTS

| | |
|---|---|
| Broadband | The term broadband refers to a telecommunications signal or device of greater bandwidth, in some sense, than another standard or usual signal or device (and the broader the band, the greater the capacity for traffic). |
| | Different criteria for 'broad' have been applied in different contexts and at different times. Its origin is in physics, acoustics and radio systems engineering, where it had been used with a meaning similar to wideband. |
| FINANCIAL | FINANCIAL is the weekly English-language newspaper with offices in Tbilisi, Georgia and Kiev, Ukraine. Published by Intelligence Group LLC, FINANCIAL is focused on opinion leaders and top business decision-makers; It's about world's largest companies, investing, careers, and small business. It is distributed in Georgia and Ukraine. |
| Othello error | Othello error occurs when a suspicious observer discounts cues of truthfulness, given the observer's need to conform his/her observations of suspicions of deception. Essentially Othello error occurs 'when the lie catcher fails to consider that a truthful person who is under stress may appear to be lying.' (Ekman, 1985). |
| | The term relates to the Shakespeare play in which Othello misinterprets Desdemona's reaction to Cassio's death. |
| Procedural | A Procedural is a cross-genre type of literature, film, or television program involving a sequence of technical detail. A documentary film may be written in a procedural style to heighten narrative interest. |
| | Types |
| | Television |
| | Fiction |
| | In television, 'procedural' specifically refers to a genre of programs in which a problem is introduced, investigated and solved all within the same episode. |
| Exposition Boy | Exposition Boy is a colloquialism from television fandom and fan fiction which identifies the character who seems to be there mostly to allow the writer to explain things which there is no other easy way to explain. These can be plot points, or the inner thoughts of the other characters, which are revealed to the audience when they tell them to this character. |

# Chapter 12. Deceptive Communication

## CHAPTER HIGHLIGHTS & NOTES: KEY TERMS, PEOPLE, PLACES, CONCEPTS

| | |
|---|---|
| Clubflyer | A Clubflyer or flyer (also spelled flier or called handbill) is a single page leaflet advertising a nightclub, event, service, community communication. |
| Restrictive | In semantics, a modifier is said to be restrictive (or defining) if it restricts the reference of its head. For example, in 'the red car is fancier than the blue one', red and blue are restrictive, because they restrict which cars car and one are referring to. ('The car is fancier than the one' would make little sense). |
| Perjury | Perjury, is the willful act of swearing a false oath or affirmation to tell the truth, whether spoken or in writing, concerning matters material to a judicial proceeding. That is, the witness falsely promises to tell the truth about matters which affect the outcome of the case. For example, it is not considered perjury to lie about one's age unless age is a factor in determining the legal result, such as eligibility for old age retirement benefits. |
| E-mail | Electronic mail, often abbreviated as email or E-mail, is a method of exchanging digital messages, designed primarily for human use. E-mail systems are based on a store-and-forward model in which E-mail computer server systems accept, forward, deliver and store messages on behalf of users, who only need to connect to the E-mail infrastructure, typically an E-mail server, with a network-enabled device (e.g., a personal computer) for the duration of message submission or retrieval. Rarely is E-mail transmitted directly from one user's device to another's. |
| Online | The terms online and offline (also on-line and off-line) have specific meanings with respect to computer technology and telecommunication. In general, 'online' indicates a state of connectivity, while 'offline' indicates a disconnected state. In common usage, 'online' often refers to the Internet or the World Wide Web. |
| Diversity | In sociology and political studies, the term diversity (or diverse) is used to describe political entities (neighborhoods, student bodies, etc) with members who have identifiable differences in their cultural backgrounds or lifestyles.<br><br>The term describes differences in racial or ethnic classifications, age, gender, religion, philosophy, physical abilities, socioeconomic background, sexual orientation, gender identity, intelligence, mental health, physical health, genetic attributes, behavior, attractiveness, or other identifying features.<br><br>In measuring human diversity, a diversity index measures the probability that any two residents, chosen at random, would be of different ethnicities. |
| Communication | Communication is the activity of conveying information. Communication has been derived from the Latin word 'communis', meaning to share. |

# Chapter 12. Deceptive Communication

CHAPTER HIGHLIGHTS & NOTES: KEY TERMS, PEOPLE, PLACES, CONCEPTS

| | |
|---|---|
| Dissimulation | Dissimulation is a form of deception in which one conceals the truth. It consists of concealing the truth, or in the case of half-truths, concealing parts of the truth, like inconvenient or secret information. Dissimulation differs from simulation, in which one exhibits false information. |
| Equivocation | Equivocation is classified as both a formal and informal fallacy. It is the misleading use of a term with more than one meaning or sense . <br><br> It is often confused with amphiboly; however, Equivocation is ambiguity arising from the misleading use of a word and amphiboly is ambiguity arising from misleading use of punctuation or syntax. |
| Filler | In linguistics, a filler is a sound or word that is spoken in conversation by one participant to signal to others that he/she has paused to think but is not yet finished speaking. These are not to be confused with placeholder names, such as thingamajig, which refer to objects or people whose names are temporarily forgotten, irrelevant, or unknown. Different languages have different characteristic filler sounds; in English, the most common filler sounds are uh /?/, er /?/ and um /?m/. |
| Psychoanalytic literary criticism | Psychoanalytic literary criticism refers to literary criticism which, in method, concept, theory is influenced by the tradition of psychoanalysis begun by Sigmund Freud. Psychoanalytic reading has been practiced since the early development of psychoanalysis itself, and has developed into a rich and heterogeneous interpretive tradition. <br><br> It is a literary approach where critics see the text as if it were a kind of dream. |
| Speech error | Speech errors, commonly referred to as slips of the tongue, are conscious or unconscious deviations from the apparently intended form of an utterance. They can be subdivided into spontaneously and inadvertently produced speech errors and intentionally produced word-plays or puns. Another distinction can be drawn between production and comprehension errors. |
| Interpersonal deception theory | Interpersonal deception theory attempts to explain the manner in which individuals deal with actual or perceived deception on the conscious and subconscious levels while engaged in face-to-face communication. Communication is not static; it is influenced not only by one's own goals, but also by the context of the interaction as it unfolds. The sender's conduct and messages are affected by conduct and messages of the receiver, and vice versa. |

# Chapter 12. Deceptive Communication

**CHAPTER QUIZ: KEY TERMS, PEOPLE, PLACES, CONCEPTS**

1. _____ occurs when a suspicious observer discounts cues of truthfulness, given the observer's need to conform his/her observations of suspicions of deception. Essentially _____ occurs 'when the lie catcher fails to consider that a truthful person who is under stress may appear to be lying.' (Ekman, 1985).

   The term relates to the Shakespeare play in which Othello misinterprets Desdemona's reaction to Cassio's death.

   a. Out-group homogeneity
   b. Overjustification effect
   c. Othello error
   d. Digital

2. _____ is a colloquialism from television fandom and fan fiction which identifies the character who seems to be there mostly to allow the writer to explain things which there is no other easy way to explain. These can be plot points, or the inner thoughts of the other characters, which are revealed to the audience when they tell them to this character.

   In first-person detective shows, the lead is usually _____, and the concept is less necessary (and less clear).

   a. It was a dark and stormy night
   b. Opening narration
   c. Out of character
   d. Exposition Boy

3. _____ is a form of deception in which one conceals the truth. It consists of concealing the truth, or in the case of half-truths, concealing parts of the truth, like inconvenient or secret information. _____ differs from simulation, in which one exhibits false information.

   a. Dropout
   b. Dissimulation
   c. Facilitated communication
   d. Factlet

4. In linguistics, a filler is a sound or word that is spoken in conversation by one participant to signal to others that he/she has paused to think but is not yet finished speaking. These are not to be confused with placeholder names, such as thingamajig, which refer to objects or people whose names are temporarily forgotten, irrelevant, or unknown. Different languages have different characteristic _____ sounds; in English, the most common _____ sounds are uh /?/, er /?/ and um /?m/.

   a. John Rupert Firth
   b. Foregrounding
   c. Filler
   d. Gesamtbedeutung

## Chapter 12. Deceptive Communication

CHAPTER QUIZ: KEY TERMS, PEOPLE, PLACES, CONCEPTS

5. The term _____ refers to a telecommunications signal or device of greater bandwidth, in some sense, than another standard or usual signal or device (and the broader the band, the greater the capacity for traffic).

Different criteria for 'broad' have been applied in different contexts and at different times. Its origin is in physics, acoustics and radio systems engineering, where it had been used with a meaning similar to wideband.

a. Digital call quality
b. Camcon Binary Actuator
c. Digital clock
d. Broadband

**ANSWER KEY**
Chapter 12. Deceptive Communication

1. c
2. d
3. b
4. c
5. d

## You can take the complete Chapter Practice Test

### for Chapter 12. Deceptive Communication
on all key terms, persons, places, and concepts.

## Online 99 Cents

### http://www.epub21.1.20820.12.cram101.com/

Use www.Cram101.com for all your study needs

including Cram101's online interactive problem solving labs in

chemistry, statistics, mathematics, and more.

## Other Cram101 e-Books and Tests

**Want More?**
**Cram101.com...**

**Cram101.com provides the outlines and highlights of your textbooks, just like this e-StudyGuide, but also gives you the PRACTICE TESTS, and other exclusive study tools for all of your textbooks.**

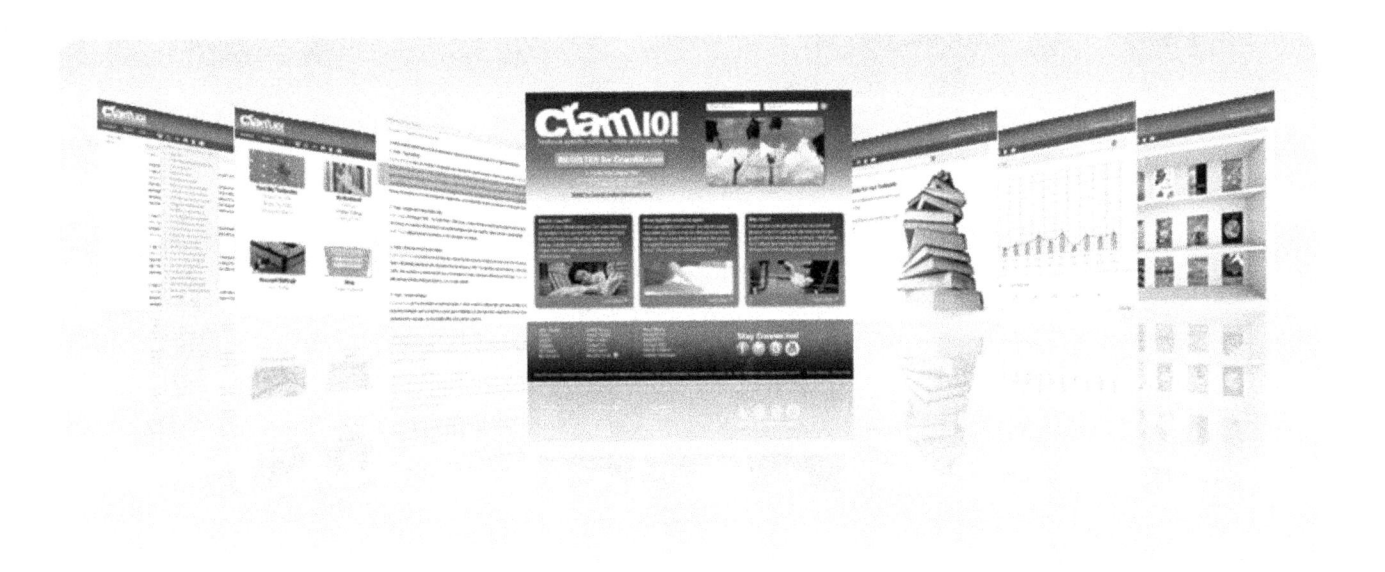

**Learn More. *Just click***
***http://www.cram101.com/***

CPSIA information can be obtained
at www.ICGtesting.com
Printed in the USA
FSHW021337100521
81304FS